"As a mediocre golfer far along the back nine of life I had largely soured on my increasing paucity of talent. Then along came Tripp Bowden, who persuaded me to tell the story of one of the few peaks in a career played largely in troughs and valleys.

"I had the greatest fun dredging the memory bank to come up with the story of one marvelous day in my golfing life as an underachiever. Those fond memories reminded me so vividly that everyone's golf game, however puny, should always be enjoyed. Thank you, Tripp, and what a fine collection of tales you have assembled."

—**Ben Wright, Longtime PGA Tour Television Commentator and Analyst**

"A poignant collection of golf stories, full of wisdom. In a golf world that has become obsessed with numbers and ratings, Tripp Bowden delightfully reminds us that having fun is the reason we play the game: it is the *experience* that we should savor, indeed. *All the Memorable Rounds* captures the essence of the game, and it is ultimately a story about love."

—**John Sabino, Author of *Golf's Iron Horse***

"*All the Memorable Rounds* is an eclectic collection of golf—and life—stories told from every lens. Tripp Bowden not only takes his readers through a memorable journey of golf, but also through a delightful ride in life. He shares head-nodding, heart-felt analogies we can all relate to; no matter what season we are in our lives, or in our golf game. This book will touch your soul."

—**Dr. Gina Smith, Professor, Arizona State University**

"*All the Memorable Rounds* is an intriguing mix of inspirational and motivational stories and memoirs that incorporates humor, drama, and passion throughout. Tripp Bowden brings the virtues of golfing heroes and others to life from the perspective of an experienced golfer and caddy. The author's vivid descriptions of the various and finest golf courses provide interesting data as well as tips applicable to everyone. Through these memoirs, Bowden illustrates that those who work hard and play hard have the opportunity to realize their dreams, as depicted by his first hole-in-one at the young age of twelve, when Tripp's child-like love of the game willed that little white golf ball into the hole. What a beautiful book."

—Joyce Rector, Former CEO of PlanGraphics, Inc.

"Our college philosophy professor often told us, 'You can't step in the same river twice.' But the way Tripper has stored away all these memories (like that half-eaten cheeseburger he pulled out on #6 at The Hills), he takes us right back to some old delightful streams. What a gift!"

—Vic Baker, Sales Representative, Stafford Nut and Bolt

"Bobby Jones said, 'Golf is the closest game to the game we call life.' *All the Memorable Rounds* is a wonderful collection of game of life stories that is sure to trigger in all of us our own personal moments when golf and life kissed each other."

—Doc Bowden, Surgeon, Episcopal Priest, and Masters Historian

"This book captures the essence of what golf is supposed to be…FUN! Bowden's tales will inspire you to play the game with friends, with laughter in your bag. This book is a delightful walk through the eyes of golfers who simply love to play the game."

—Ethan Andrews, Marine Corps Lt. Col. Huey Pilot

"Tripp Bowden is to golf what Bill Bryson is to the Appalachian Trail. Somehow, he puts you in the presence of living legends, from Ben Crenshaw to Dr. J to Julia Roberts, and regular folks too, with an easy style that makes time disappear as you lose yourself in the moments he shares."

—Brett Clemmer, Tripp's Friend and President of Man in the Mirror, Inc.

"As a non-golfer, I began reading Tripp Bowden's latest book, *All the Memorable Rounds*, with dubious curiosity about the potential literary appeal of golfing memories. I soon found myself an adventurer, passing through portals revealing compelling tales, humorous anecdotes, personal insights, and physical beauty. Bowden is an accomplished purveyor of the mysteries of human nature, flawed yet inspired."

—Jane Savage, Educator

ALL THE MEMORABLE ROUNDS

Golf Adventures and Misadventures,
from Augusta National to
Cypress Point and Beyond

Tripp Bowden

with a little help from his friends

Foreword by Dr. Bob Jones IV

Skyhorse Publishing

Skyhorse Publishing books may be purchased in bulk at special discounts for sales promotion, corporate gifts, fund-raising, or educational purposes. Special editions can also be created to specifications. For details, contact the Special Sales Department, Skyhorse Publishing, 307 West 36th Street, 11th Floor, New York, NY 10018 or info@skyhorsepublishing.com.

Skyhorse® and Skyhorse Publishing® are registered trademarks of Skyhorse Publishing, Inc.®, a Delaware corporation.

Visit our website at www.skyhorsepublishing.com.

10 9 8 7 6 5 4 3 2 1

Library of Congress Cataloging-in-Publication Data is available on file.

Chapter-opening illustrations courtesy of iStock.

Cover design by Tom Lau
Cover photo credit: iStock

ISBN: 978-1-5107-1486-1
Ebook ISBN: 978-1-5107-1487-8
Printed in China

For my wife, Fletch, who still believes in me in spite of my many misgivings, and for our magical kiddos Arrie B and Holly Mac, who still think their Daddy hung the moon.
If only I could reach that far.

"When a seed first finds soil, every piece of dirt matters."

—My good friend and late-night philosopher, Billy D, who gets the game like I do, circa 1987, Wheeler Road, Augusta, Georgia.

Insight for the ages, golf or otherwise.

Contents

Contents

Foreword

No game of which I am aware is as baffling as the game of golf. It is a game that is more than five centuries old and yet it thrives on modern technology. It is a social game, yet it can be played alone. It is a composite of eighteen holes, yet it is made up of individual shots. It is an athletic endeavor that is often played by the most unathletic people imaginable. It is a game that lives in the sepia images of golfers long past while at the same time thriving in an HD world. For all of these apparent contradictions, what is it that makes this royal and ancient game so appealing, that draws its adherents to it like a moth to flame?

On first blush, it may be the equipment. Golfers are always looking for that next driver that will promise them that extra ten yards. They are waiting for the wedge that claims that no balls will be left in the sandtrap or skulled over the back of the green. The putter that will eliminate the dreaded three-putt. This quest for mechanical perfection is as old as the game itself. In fact, more than a half-century ago, my grandfather, Bobby Jones, had Spalding make a custom set of clubs for President Eisenhower, an enthusiastic golfer. The President wrote a thank-you note to my grandfather but complained that his golf was no better with the new equipment. Bub, my family's nickname for my grandfather, wrote back, "Dear Mr. President, Sometimes one has to recognize that the fault lies with the Indian, not with the Arrow. Sincerely, Bob." No, the appeal of golf does not lie in the implements of the game.

Maybe the answer to golf's appeal lies in its great tournaments. The four majors and a few other tournaments have provided excitement and memories that fill volumes. The championship courses of the world, from Augusta National to Winged Foot, and all in between are as familiar to the average golfer as his or her own track. Yet, for all that familiarity, average golfers can no more appreciate the pressure of championship golf than they can appreciate the feel of the lunar surface under their feet.

What is the answer to the question of golf's appeal? The book that you hold in your hands, I think, begins to answer that question. The appeal of the game of golf lies first and foremost in the golf courses where the game is played. Great courses such as Augusta National and lesser courses, too. Courses that are on the *Golf Digest Top 100* and courses that no one outside of town has ever heard of. These courses are the canvas on which the brush strokes of our great game are painted.

But what is the paint? I submit that the paint is the relationships that are formed in the game, the shared shots and shared memories that provide connections between men and women who might otherwise never know each other. My friend Tripp Bowden has put together with his friends a series of essays about what makes this game of ours so special. As you read the stories collected in this book, you will discover some places that are gems. But what will most stand out is the relationships, first, between people and golf courses. Most importantly, what you will discover are some of the people who make the game great. They're not necessarily the professionals. Sometimes they are ordinary folks. But these people are the ones who add the texture to the game that make it so memorable. So, whether you play at a championship venue or the local municipal track, take time to savor this book, remember all of those who have made this game so meaningful to you, and raise a glass to this great game that connects us wherever we may be.

—Dr. Bob Jones IV
Atlanta, Georgia

Photo by Kim Fletcher Bowden

Introduction

MEMORIES FOR THE NURSING HOME

What makes a golf course great?

Is it the course rating, the stimp, the stroke index, the slope rating (God forbid), the layout, or the gorgeous clubhouse with the wraparound porch and columns extending to the sky?

Is it the year the course was built, the designer, the granite countertops in the bathrooms, or the pristine condition of the course, with bunker sand soft as flour?

No, no, no. A thousand times no.

It is the *experience.*

It is the experience that defines a golf course, the experience that makes *that* round of golf, and that golf course you just played, one for the memory books, not just one for the credit card bill. It is the experience from the parking lot to the pro shop, the golf course to the caddies, the 1st tee jitters to the 18th tee with all bets on the line, and you're as pumped as a jumpy castle.

It's the 19th hole, commiserating over a pint over the ones that got away, raising a glass to the ones that didn't.

It's talking with your caddy over a putt that just *has* to break a cup to the left, but he says, "No, Boss, it's straight as a first grade pencil," and then he pops you on the shoulder and says, "Soon as your knees stop shaking, knock it *straight* in the cup!" And he's right as rain on both counts.

The shaking *and* the breaking.

It's holding court with the cat that shines your shoes, both your golf and street ones, with a shine that shames a diamond, so you slip him an extra Lincoln, and he smiles because you get it. Yeah, man, you get it.

It's having an after-round cold one while the high school kid who wipes down your clubs asks where you're from and you tell him, and you ask him where he's from, and you realize you're from the same damn town, even though you're a thousand miles from home.

It's chatting up Ms. Betty at the halfway house, and she is steady rocking the bouffant, even though it's the 90s, but Ms. Betty doesn't care. Ms. Betty serves up the best dang chili dog in the South—cooked slow and low, on a bun so steamy that dog is hard to hold onto, but she's serving up the truth.

Damn, this is a good dog.

Ms. Betty calls you *Darlin'* and *Shugah* and you would stuff a few extra dollars in her tip jar if she had one, so instead you just slide 'em on the counter and smile. Not because she called you *Darlin'* or the chili dog was one for the ages, but because she reminds you of your momma. On the way home, you call your momma and tell her about your day and that you love her.

Why?

Because it is *all* about the experience.

It's about learning, living, and loving the history of a course like Shady Oaks in Fort Worth, Texas, through the eyes of the cart boy who once called a trailer park home. Now he's twenty-three, putting himself through med school by working the cart barn at the legendary Ben Hogan's only golf course design, the place where Hogan spent his still youthful retirement days, and would one afternoon swing his game-changing sticks for the very last time. It's where Hogan had his own private table in the grill room, by the big bay window overlooking the 18th green and the 1st tee, where he would sit for hours watching groups start and finish their round, minding their time on his wrist watch. It's where the head pro would give lessons to members, guests— even the cart boy from the trailer park.

The experience is playing a round at Palmetto Golf Club, in Aiken, South Carolina, just off Whiskey Road—a fitting name considering you're playing with your group of blood brothers from back in the day that are still with you to *this* day, who love the game in the spirit of Chi-Chi and Trevino, even though they couldn't break 80 with a sledge hammer.

Even if John Henry was slinging it.

It's where you learn Palmetto was built in 1892, as a three-hole golf course with three sets of tees played two times each to equal 18 holes on greens made of sand because the money ran out, even though the course was built for famous, wealthy Northerners who wintered in Aiken. That was where the tracks ended for the train coming from New York. It was a long horse and buggy ride to Florida back then.

Palmetto members such as Sears, Rockefeller, Goodyear, and Milburn soon became members of Augusta National Golf Club, built in the 1930s. When these Palmetto members asked Bobby Jones and Cliff Roberts to kindly send over their designer, a gentleman named Alister MacKenzie who came all the way across the Pond from Scotland, to finish the Palmetto and makc her a proper 18-hole golf course, Bobby and Cliff said yes.

Alister MacKenzie. Perhaps the greatest golf course designer of all time.

When you play Palmetto, you see the designer's fingerprints at every turn—you hit every club in your bag, you four-putt at least once on the signature 5th hole, and you can't believe how long the short holes play. She's only 6,100 yards from the tips, but she plays longer than a bad blind date.

Along with the experience, there's the proverbial cart boy who's not really a boy, but a gentleman in his 60s named John Williams, who put four kids through college by working sixteen-hour days at the Palmetto for thirty-plus years. The same man who will later greet your group on the 10th tee with hot dogs all the way, packs of Planters Peanuts, bags of Lay's Potato Chips, Cokes in the can, and cold beers on ice, because there is no halfway house at Palmetto.

Back in 1892, there was no such thing as "a snack bar at the turn," and Palmetto keeps with tradition. There will *never* be a snack bar at the turn at Palmetto, and that is a beautiful thing.

One more experience to mention. It's about playing a local Augusta, Georgia, muni known as the Cabbage Patch, legendarily dubbed such because Red Douglas, the head pro for over 40 years, grew a tiny vegetable garden adjacent to the tenth tee, and he was of Irish descent, so, naturally, there was cabbage in the ground. Red would let you play the course for whatever you had in your pocket, and he would ask,

"What'cha got in there, son?"—a nickel, twenty-five cents, a dollar—Mr. Red didn't care, he just wanted you, you and every kid who loved the game like he did, to have a chance to play. The locals might say the nickname came from the fairways, so bumpy they were as if he had planted those cabbages and not Bermuda grass from tee to green on every hole!

So, what makes a golf course experience *great?*

Is it playing a round of golf at that same Cabbage Patch with the younger son of your mom's best friend—a nine-year-old kid who'd *never* played the game before, who takes tremendous pride in circling bogeys on his scorecard, even though he only made *two*, two more than he should have?

Who in the hell circles bogeys?

This kid would go on to serve our country as a damn fine Marine, become a Lt. Colonel, piloting Hueys, flying rescue missions, in Afghanistan and above roofs and trees in the 5th Ward after Hurricane Katrina.

If only he could rescue his golf game! That kid and I would become best friends, and for the record, he still circles bogeys with a broken pencil he sharpens with a beat-up Buck Knife.

Y'all, great golf is all about the *experience*, not a slope rating.

Let's remove the numbers and have some fun.

Chapter 1

SO THEN BEN SAYS
TO CHARLIE, "CHARLIE,
MEET MY FRIEND TRIPP."

Bush Field Airport, Augusta, Georgia, 15.7 miles from Augusta National Golf Club

By Tripp Bowden

It's Sunday evening, April 9, 1995, the air soft and breezy, and another magical Masters is in the books. Unfathomable might be the better word, because no one, not even the winner himself, expected a fairy tale ending like this. Having flown out west to Austin, Texas on Masters Week Tuesday to say a final farewell to the legendary Harvey Penick, his beloved best friend and mentor and the only golf teacher he ever had, Ben Crenshaw then flew back in to Augusta with a heavy heart and pockets just as heavy with missed cuts after missed cuts.

His life is in shambles and his game has gone to shit.

Now it's Thursday, April 6th, where we find Ben standing on the practice tee at Augusta National with his trusty caddy Carl Jackson on the bag. Carl, who has been caddying at Augusta damn near since he could walk, is arguably the best caddy at Augusta (in the 20-plus years since the aforementioned events have occurred, Carl Jackson has since retired, but he went out in a grand style, with kinfolk on Ben's bag).

Ben is botching shots left and right. For every one ball flushed off the sweet spot, the other nine are sour as crabapples.

Without warning, without being asked, as if channeling the great Harvey Penick himself, Carl spots something, something so simple, as obvious as the nose on your face.

Ball position.

Carl leans down and moves the ball back just a touch in Ben's stance—not much, but just enough to make all the difference in the world. Then he whispers: "Now take a tighter turn in your shoulders." Like flipping a switch, suddenly Ben can't miss. Suddenly every shot is flush; every ball is hit right off the screws. He feels like a kid again—like he can't miss no matter what. And so what if he does? He'll get the next one.

Though more recently a little long in the tooth and a little grey around the edges, two-time Masters Champion Ben Crenshaw's swing hasn't changed one bit—nor has his hold on the flat-blade, if I were to guess. (*Photo by Keith Allison, courtesy of Wikimedia Commons*)

And we all know he's the best putter in the game. Ben's bad days with the blade are better than most pros' good ones.

Three days and a most improbable Green Jacket later, Ben is in the office of Augusta caddy master Freddie Bennett, known far and wide as one of the best caddy masters in the game (Freddie is in the Caddy Hall of Fame), if not *the* best. Ben hands Freddie his golf glove—the same glove he had on his hand coming up 18—shaking his head and smiling.

Freddie smiles back. "Congratulations, man."

Freddie looks at me, winks, and smiles. I have had the catbird seat in his office the Sunday after Masters many a time, but this just might be the all time best.

"Thanks, Freddie. Can't believe it."

"Believe it," says Freddie, handing me the golf glove as Gentle Ben pushes the screen door open and walks out into the spotlight.

If I'd known what was going to happen next, I'd have taken that golden glove with me.

• • • •

On that same Sunday, April 9th, just a few hours removed from the most improbable championship by the most unlikely of champions, I'm with my girlfriend Ali at Bush Field Airport to pick up my mom's Fleetwood Brougham Cadillac—an old-school whale of a ride that can scat 8 people, fishing cooler full of beverages included. The wheels were on loan during the week to a house guest, some New York bond trader—a friend of a friend kind of guest. Apparently he has a private jet, because he's parked the Cadillac in that restricted area. No car, but he has his own plane?

He didn't mention anything to me about private jets, just that the keys to the Caddy would be on the left front tire.

I open the door and get out of Ali's silver Honda Accord to go grab the keys. When I look up, standing in front of me is none other than Ben Crenshaw, the just-now 1995 Masters Champion, having a cigarette outside the entrance to the hangar for the private jets. Ben's by himself, all by his lonesome, having a casual smoke, looking up into the stars between puffs. There's not a soul in sight—it's just him, Ali, and me.

Me and Ben, the Masters Champion, just hanging out at the local Augusta airport.

Normally, on the odd chance I see a celebrity up close and personal, I let them be. I've seen a few that way, standing close enough to each other we could read shirt labels. There was Billy Gibbons from ZZ TOP at the Memphis International Airport, beard rolled up like a rock 'n' roll Mennonite. Then Hall of Fame baller Dr. J (he's taller than he looks on TV) on an East Side New York street corner—the light stopped us both; I looked up and he looked down. He winked at me and grinned. Also Julia Roberts walking past my one-bedroom apartment—wearing a brown woolen skull cap of all things, looking right at me and smiling, as if to say: Thanks for not asking for my autograph.

I've also run into Luciano Pavarotti, at the McDonald's near the corner of 57th Street and 6th Ave, eating a Big Mac at 2 a.m. and scarfing down fries. I sat two tables away. I didn't ask for his autograph either.

But this feels different. I feel the call to go over, not to my mom's Cadillac but to Ben and shake his hand, and tell him, tell him, tell him what? Congrats on the win? Way to go, Gentle Ben. We were all pulling for you. What a magical moment in time!

I look back at Ali. She looks at me and nods. "You've got to do it," she says. We haven't spoken a word until now, but she knows exactly what I'm thinking.

I go over.

I go over to the Masters Champion, trying to appear like maybe I work here, coming in for the night shift, maybe running a little late because I'm walking faster than I want to. Ben looks up, smiles at me. It's more than just acknowledgement; it's a welcoming smile. As in: please, come over and say hello. And I do with hand extended, with courage I didn't know I had in me.

"Hi, Mr. Crenshaw. I'm Tripp. Tripp Bowden. That was, that was magical what you did today. You had the whole world crying right there with you when you putted out on 18 and Carl reached over to keep you from falling—what an incredibly special moment."

I don't know where these words are coming from. God, maybe?

Ben smiles, his hand still in mine. There's a big ol' lump in my throat, like I could cry again, tears running down the cheeks, right here on the spot. I can tell there's a lump in Ben's, too.

"Nice to meet you, too, Tripp. I still can't believe it. Just goes to show you anything can happen in this crazy game. Any game, for that matter."

I smile and nod my goofy noggin. Ben pulls a pack of cigs from his pocket. The brand escapes me. Marlboro Lights, maybe? Or were they Reds?

Ben offers them out. "Care for a smoke, Tripp?"

I stare at the pack of cigs like I've just seen a live dinosaur. I'm dumbfounded. Me, having a smoke with the guy who just won the Masters three hours ago?

I feel out of body.

"Uh, sure. Thanks."

I pull a cig from the pack and Ben hands me his lighter. I fire up, my hand shaking like a tractor wheel. Ben doesn't seem to notice.

"We have something in common," I say, again not knowing where the words are coming from. "The Palmetto."

"Palmetto! Man, I love that place. So much history there—I could hang out there for days."

"Me too," I say. "Pretty crazy, but the pro there taught me the game. He can barely break 80, but man can he teach."

"Tommy Moore!" says Ben. "A true ambassador of the game." Ben takes a puff and smiles. And what a great grin it is. He looks like a little kid who has just been given a big 'ol bag of lollipops.

"The best," I say, and as I go to take a puff of my own a man walks up with purpose and a quite quizzical look on his face, a face that is saying: Who in the *HELL* are you?

I recognize him from a picture in an old *Golf Magazine* issue, circa 1984. It's Charlie, Ben's older brother. I know nothing about him, but I do know he's wondering who the hell I am and what am I doing smoking a cig with his brother, the Masters Champion.

Funny . . . I'm wondering the same thing myself.

Ben speaks first. "Charlie! Where you been, man?" Charlie starts to speak, but Ben interrupts as he takes a drag off his cigarette. "Meet my friend, Tripp."

Friend? I'm your friend, too? How frikin' cool is this? "Frikin'" ain't the right word to describe this moment, but right now I can't find a better one.

Charlie and I shake hands and exchange pleasantries, mine more so than his. My cig is about to go out and so am I. But not in flames. I'm about to do something I would never do, but the moment is calling and I have to answer.

This phone will never ring again.

"Mr. Crenshaw?"

"Please, Tripp. Call me Ben. I'm just Ben."

I pull a tourist move, but with good intentions.

"Any chance I could trouble you for an autograph? Um, Ben?" I can't believe the words are coming out of my mouth.

The Masters Champion says, "Sure thing."

I tell him I'll be right back and I am, with a pen and an official Augusta National scorecard, the kind that isn't for sale. I hand both to Ben and he chuckles. "Where'd the heck'd you get this?" He holds out the scorecard like it's the Hope Diamond.

"Oh, I caddy at Augusta, straight from college to looping. Freddie hooked me up, got me the job. It's pretty cool out there—you meet a lot of interesting people."

Ben taps the pen to the scorecard, starts signing. "Freddie Bennett, another great ambassador to the game. Ol' Freddie is something else."

I nod in 100% agreement.

"Would you mind making it out to my girlfriend, Ali? She's in that car over there, the silver Honda." Ben looks over and waves. Ali waves back, no doubt stunned as I am. I spell out her name: A-l-i.

Brother Charlie eyes his watch, then me, and says, "Ben, we gotta go."

I'm thinking private jet. You can "go" whenever you want. But it's a signal, and I get it. Ben, the 1995 Masters Champion, fresh from his acceptance speech, reaches out and shakes my still shaking hand.

"It was nice to meet you, Tripp."

"Nice to meet you, too, Ben."

And just like that, he's gone. I signal to Ali that I am headed out, walk over to my mom's Caddy and into a moment frozen in time.

I learn, and not for the first time, that not all the greatest golf course experiences happen on the course.

Chapter 2

WEST LAKE
COUNTRY CLUB

Evans, Georgia

6,747 yards

By Tripp Bowden

Imagine you are me.

Imagine you are me, except you're the younger me, just a tender 10 years of age, without a worry in the world, and your mom is dropping you off at West Lake Country Club, a unique test of a track, semi-newly built on the outskirts of town, punctuated by a sea of bunkers and towering trees that love to eat Titleists and spit out the remains as deep into the woods as possible.

It's a Tuesday during the late 1970s in central Georgia, just shy of 10:00 a.m., another glorious summer rolling into your youthful life. You're fresh from week two of what will become six weeks of swim lessons at the neighborhood Brynwood Pool, where just minutes ago you mastered the dead man's float (pretty darn cool, that), treading water in the deep end for well over an hour. You quietly harbor dreams of being the

7

next Mark Spitz, the insanely talented Olympian who once won 7 gold medals in the Summer Olympic Games.

7!

But before you can take those dreams much further, you realize you are now at the golf course, and it's time to pay close attention. After all, you are quite the golfing newbie, with just a few lessons from your well-meaning dad under your belt. But you are already madly in love with the game; you've got the golf bug, the bad fever, of which there is no cure. You don't realize it, but those harbored dreams of becoming the next Mark Spitz are slowly slipping to the back burners of your life.

On tip-toed sneakers, you lean into the open window of your mom's silver Grand Ville Pontiac, thank her for the ride, and kiss her on the cheek good-bye. She hands you a couple packs of Lance Malted Peanut Butter crackers (they're cheaper than Nabisco), says drink plenty of water, Shugah, that she'll see you at dark, and just like that she's gone. You're a mama's boy (nothing wrong with that, by the way) so you can't help but feel a tiny pang of sadness when she drives away.

With your mama in the rear view mirror, you trudge across the putting green and down a gently sloping path to the West Lake driving range, where you'll be taking your first ever golf clinic under the watchful eye and tutelage of a young assistant pro by the name of Tom Moore. Tom's from Michigan, a Yankee, yet somehow seems southern to the bone. He also looks barely old enough to drive.

Tom gets it; he knows very well how to work the system, when the system needs to be worked.

The clinic lasts an hour, and it's just the basics: the grip, stance, alignment, ball position. Tom stresses the importance of these, doesn't particularly touch on the golf swing per se. Sure, you can improve upon it with instruction, make it a little better than it was before, but Tom feels strongly that you are born with your swing, that it's innate—just like you're born with your personality, your gait, the way you talk and gesture. You believe him.

Not sure why, but there's something about Tom that makes you buy all in.

If what Tom says is true, today it appears your personality is that of a dime store wooden Indian, because your knobby knees don't want to flex and your shoulders refuse to turn anywhere close to a 90-degree angle, and the Top Flite range balls scattered at your feet just a few yards from their starting point are a powerful but sad affirmation that golf is a damn hard game to learn. Mastering it seems as likely as you walking on water (which would be awfully nice if you could, seeing as you will knock many a ball into various venues of it, from lake to pond, to creek and river, even a variety of oceans over the course of your golfing life).

Mark Spitz would be proud.

But the young buck pro from Michigan doesn't seem the least bit concerned, much less worried, about the sad state of your golf swing. Tom is, however, a bit concerned that you have *never* stepped foot on an actual golf course (Putt-Putt doesn't count). You, with scratched up clubs strapped to your back but in a pretty nice golf bag, scuffed high-top Reebok tennis shoes on your Tom and Jerry's, and a used, too-big-for-you white FootJoy golf glove bunched up on your shaking left hand.

"I think you're ready," Tom says, a sly but not really trying to be sly grin on his tan, round face.

Ready for what?

Tom speaks in a bit of a whisper, as if he doesn't want the other kids to hear, so you lean in, and Tom says he thinks you have that something special in you, in spite of the dribblers, duffs, tops, and chunks you've been sacrificing to the golf gods for the past 60 minutes. But you *did* flush a couple—well, make that one—and you *did* get that magical feeling of the golf ball just getting in the way of your swing. You heard the click, the crack of bat on ball, but all you felt was swing.

Again, you believe the young pro from Michigan. Let's go one better: you believe *in* him.

Very different things.

Tom motions up the hill, away from the range. He's pointing to the golf course, a foreign land for you, then looks you square in the eyes and says, "How 'bout you go and play a few holes? Take what we just did here, and take it out there." Once again he points to the golf course, but he's pointing to the right. The far right.

The back 9, not the front.

There's a staunch rule at West Lake stating unaccompanied junior golfers can only play the course at certain times during the week (who made that rule I'll never know), and *never* during the weekend. This is *not* one of those certain times. But for Tom, rules such as these are made to be broken, and if not broken, *bent*, if only just a little.

Tom walks over to his no-topper golf cart, you hop in, and off you go.

"Say, how's about a little refreshment?" Tom says, as you head up the hill.

"Sure," you answer. "That'd be great. Thanks!"

Tom zips up the hill to the pro shop, slips quietly inside and into the men's locker room, and returns with two sloshing Cokes and an overflowing cup of Charles' Pretzels, covered in rock salt and big as your fist.

Just who the heck *is* this guy?

The young pro from Michigan smiles, hands over the sloshing *soda* (as they say up north) and pretzels and rolls the cart out onto West Lake's back 9, pedal to the floor and the wind in your hair. Tom pays no mind to stopping at the 10th tee, for obvious reasons. You both know the West Lake rules for junior golfers. Tom doesn't stop at the 11th tee, either.

"The head pro lives right over there," says Tom, pointing to a rather sprawling brick ranch that seems flush to the tee box. He shakes his head as if to say, "You get me?" You nod as if to say, "Oh, do I ever!"

Your journey ends at the 12th, a beast of a par 4 with dramatic elevation changes and a forty-yard-deep green with mountainous slopes. Tom drops you off at the red tees—what he calls the beginner tees, even though they are actually the tees for the ladies. Keep in mind this is 1976, and there is no such thing as junior tees, or kids' tees.

"Start here," says Tom. "We'll jump back there when the time is right." He points to the white tees some 40 yards behind us, and then casually tosses over a pack of tees and a sleeve of balls.

Brand new Titleists!

"Got it," you say, watching as Tom drives off towards the 12th green instead of back the way you came.

You turn to the vast fairway stretching out in front of you. It looks like miles to the green, not yards.

Your very first time on an actual golf course with clubs in hand, though, technically, it still won't be your very first round of golf—you skipped the first eleven and

now you're only playing seven. But that first round will come soon, I promise. For now, it's just you and West Lake, and not a soul in sight. Got the place all to yourself on a beautiful summertime Tuesday morning, though by now the sun is starting to get angry, throwing bright, hot darts into the ground. But all you can feel right now is the game of golf, and man does it feel great.

Life-changing great, like nothing you've ever felt before.

• • • •

West Lake will be an enchanted place for you and the game to grow up together. There will be late afternoon rounds with your dad, your hero, even though you don't really believe in heroes, at least not the hero-worshipping side of things. Your dad will become a very accomplished surgeon, always busy, busy cutting and teaching while learning and perfecting his craft, though the game of golf will become the perfect conduit for precious time shared between father and son.

If it weren't for the game of golf, you likely would have never known your dad at all.

But thanks to golf, you will grow to know your dad well, and your time together will be filled with countless evening rounds of 18 holes played in well under two hours, your best friend and dog since childhood Geraldine in tow. She's funny, that pup—often chilling in the golf cart when your game is good, or taking off down a random fairway when your game goes south, as if she can somehow tell a snap hook from a stripe. But there is no doubt Geraldine knows when you are stinking it up.

Don't ask me how, she just does.

There will be a hole-in-one the summer you turn twelve, a swung-with-all-your-might driver from the ladies' tees on the par 3 8th, from a whopping 142 yards out, the ball rolling through the bunker and into the cup like it has eyes! There's a kid hanging out in the oak tree guarding the green, and in his excitement of seeing your hole-in-one he falls out, bouncing off the grass like a sack of pecans. You might have heard of him, or at least his music: the kid is Charles Kelley, lead singer and guitarist for Grammy Award-winning country music group *Lady Antebellum*.

Small world.

My dog, Geraldine. We were puppies together, she and I. Geraldine loved to hang out in our golf cart as Pop and I tried our best to navigate our no-playing asses around West Lake Country Club. (*Photo courtesy of Joe Bowden*)

Your dad falls to the ground, too, but unlike Charles he falls on purpose, having never had an ace before, and in fact it will be some 25 years more before he does. Your dad (you call him Pop) slaps the turf, laughing to beat the band and yells, with a pause between each word: "Son-of-a-bitch!"

You smile, with little idea what that phrase means, having led a pretty clean life up to this point. You also have little idea what you just accomplished, but it must be pretty special because your dad walks over and hugs you so tight it hurts, but in a very good way. The sun is setting and it is time to go home. But it is also time to come back. You come back the next day, to make the round official, otherwise the ace won't count. You gotta play all 18 holes. That's the rule.

You gotta play all 18, or as they say in baseball: *You gotta touch 'em all!*

• • • •

On the back nine the next evening, your dad darn near aces the 13th, a booger-bear of a par 3 with ball-eating bunkers and overhanging pine trees that don't favor your angle to a far-tucked pin. Pop's ball is hanging on the edge, just a quarter turn from falling in.

Actually, let's call it a dime.

The rule is you have 10 seconds upon approach to deem your ball stationary with no chance to drop into the hole. For you and your dad, those 10 seconds seem like 10 days, but still the ball doesn't move.

The ace for Doc comes off the score card. A leaner for an ace on the 13th! Damn, damn, damn! (Those are your Pop's words, not yours.)

You finish up and pull into the cart barn, the evening over, one grin maybe bigger than the other—you might be able to guess whose is which—but your ace is now official. To your surprise, Tom is there, with a complete set of golf clubs in his thick hands. A complete set of forged Hogans, cut down to fit your diminutive size, re-gripped and ready to go!

Tommy looks down at you and smiles. "These are for you, Tripp. Play 'em until you outgrow 'em, and then pay 'em forward, ok?"

You have no idea what that means, although you will soon come to learn. All you know right now is you have a new set of clubs! You muffle out a "thank-you" and walk out into the sunset with your new set of sticks, and a brand new way of looking at the game of golf.

Thirty years later, that Hogan wedge is still in your bag.

• • • •

There is more. There's always more, if you know where to look.

There's winning the Junior Club Championship at age 15 by half a dozen shots, being dubbed "Mr. Consistency" by the local *Augusta Chronicle* press, back when a pair of 75s on a long and winding track like West Lake meant something.

There will be a victory in the Men's Club Championship, too, a three-day "W" that culminates with your best friend on your bag and a flushed three-iron on the par 3 4th from 190 yards out into a green narrow as a New York Strip. You're the only one in your group to hit that intimidating green—no one else so much as scares it—yet that seemingly simple act of hitting a ball onto a green, with the pressure cooker whistling to beat the band, tells you and your caddy that this party is over.

Sorry boys, you're playing for second (the "boys" are actually grown men in their 40s).

The following season, another grown man, who just happens to be the Club President, will fight fervently for your right to defend your championship (there are quite a few complaints that a "non-dues-paying member," a.k.a. a kid like me, took home the title). That man will win this fight, even though you won't win the title again, being a little off your game en route to a 4th-place finish.

But that's OK.

You come of age at West Lake Country Club, from Slim Jims at the turn, to New England clam chowder in the grill room, washing down that decadent chowder with glass after glass of sweet southern tea garnished with lemons over a bed of shaved ice—the glass tall as your outstretched hand. The summertime Friday junior tourneys, with trophies engraved in block letters with the corresponding PGA event, be it the Colonial or the John Deere Classic. You'll win your share of these, peacock-proud when you show your shiny spoils to mom and dad, but the wins you'll cherish the most are the times with your dad playing in the Father/Son 9-hole tournaments.

These nail-biting, 9-hole events are played in various formats, including the dastardly, father/son relationship-testing alternate shot format, where, try as you might, you are forever snatching your dad's beautifully placed tee shot on the par 4 7th hole dead-left hard, and I mean *hard*, sailing it over the Mickey Mouse ear-shaped bunker, the ball bouncing onto the hardpan as if the ground had been paved, before settling dead-ass stymie behind a towering loblolly pine and into an absolute shit of a lie.

Sorry, Pop.

You and your dad are always paired with Sweatin' Swanny and his young son, David, with Swanny big as a buffalo, sweating buckets and swilling Miller Lites faster than you could pour 'em down the drain! The pro always pairs y'all together, just in case ol' Sweatin' Swanny takes a knee (or two!) in the sweltering summer sun, and needs code blue medical assistance from your dad, the surgeon.

A miracle in and of itself, this somehow never happens.

• • • •

As you come of age at West Lake, you will hit so many practice balls your calluses will have calluses, and you'll have difficulty making a fist, your fingers so swollen and thick from use. Lucky for you, you're a lover not a fighter—at least you will be down the road.

With those hard-earned calluses comes rapid improvement in your golf game. The same goes for your dad, as he gets as low as a 2, while you get all the way down to *scratch*. There will be vast rewards for all your hard work, such as appearances in State Amateurs and US Amateur qualifiers, a full scholarship ride to local Augusta College, where you garner honors such as Freshman of the Year and Most Improved as a Fifth-Year Senior (think about that one for a moment; actually, don't).

You will even make it as far as the final stage of the 1985 British Open qualifier, where you'll sit on a locker room bench next to future Golf Hall of Famer Nick Price and chat briefly about the upcoming final round. Your dad likes to joke (and it's a good one): "Sitting on that bench next to Nick Price was as close as you ever got to the PGA Tour!"

Your memories of your days at West Lake are mighty powerful, chock full of the brand of the vim and vigor that only comes from youth.

But no memory is more powerful than your mom dropping you off for that very first golf clinic with Tommy, the Michigan pro, which quickly turned one-on-one, with you clutching malt crackers in one very nervous right hand, balancing yourself with the other as you lean in to your mom for a see-you-later kiss on the cheek. You watch as she slowly drives away, and you can't help feeling that part of you is driving away with her.

What you wouldn't give for a return trip.

Chapter 3

ARCADIA BLUFFS GOLF COURSE

Arcadia, Michigan

7,300 yards

By Tim Gaffney, engineer, hard as that is to believe for those who knew me in my youth

When my business partner Tom Lamasters first told me we had landed the vaunted Michigan Oil contract, I was extremely excited about the opportunity to work on their oil production issues, knowing we had just the product to solve them.

But there is a caveat, and it has to do with consistency.

Northern Michigan oil wells produce a very different type of oil than what you see in the media: it is brown, thick, and heavy, more like tapioca pudding than oil. Michigan oil is far from Texas sweet crude, but our company's product was just the solution to solve all their problems and then some. This stuff works wonders.

That said, I was less than excited about the prospect of traveling to the state of Michigan in wintertime to address their pudding problem. My lovely bride was born and raised there, and I had spent more than a couple of frostbitten weeks in that state during the wooing and courting. A few days housebound, and you start to sympathize with Jack Nicholson—Heeeerrrrrre's Johnny!

So instead, I took every opportunity to tailor my business travel arrangements to place me in lovely Northern Michigan during the summertime. I quickly discovered that all that chest-deep snow magically melts into a lush green countryside, creating a vacation haven for many, and a golfing Mecca for the rest of us.

My golf bag soon became standard luggage for those business trips.

During one of our first ventures to the land of tapioca and honey, two of my business partners and I traveled deep into the seemingly endless woods off the two-lane M-15 to visit one of our clients' many wellheads. We were to meet a well foreman named Don Brandt regarding an issue with our chemical injection system that apparently had a leaking o-ring. We arrived a little early, and one of my partners fired up a cig as we waited. About that time, Don arrived on the scene. He jumped out of his Dodge pickup truck like it was on fire, stormed over to my partner, and demanded in no uncertain terms he put out the cigarette. Somewhat shaken, I tried to stabilize the situation by providing this very angry man some literature on our product (just what the doctor ordered, right?). As I opened the trunk of my car, he noticed our three sets of golf clubs. Instantly, the conversation turned. Don was far more interested in where we were playing that week than any of the sales literature I had to offer.

So in lieu of getting our asses kicked all the way back to Arizona, we had met a kindred spirit, a fellow lover of the game of golf, and now that we spoke the same language, we spent the next two afternoons playing remote Michigan golf with Don Brandt as our very capable Sherpa.

It was the beginning of a beautiful, and lifelong, friendship.

Within a few summers, I had the opportunity to play golf with all of our clients in the Michigan area. Business was very good, and the vast array of lush golf courses offered the perfect venue to build friendships. You spend 4-plus hours with someone time and time again, you'll damn sure know what makes them tick, and if they're a watch worth wearing.

· · · ·

Given the long harsh winters and short golf seasons, you'd assume these northern boys to be hackers and incapable of breaking 90 with a sack of hammers. But that's as far from the truth as saying the world is flat. These guys, every damn one of them, can flat out *play*.

My close friend and client, Tom Heller, helped me better understand the secret of these Michigan ringers. Even though their golf seasons are short, they can put a peg in the ground until 9:30 at night during the summer. In fact, it's not uncommon for them to play 54 holes a day—do *that* math real quick! So by mid-June these boys are back in full form. And Tom shared another trick he uses to keep his swing in fine form. In the heart of the brutal winter, he tees up tennis balls and hits them into a snow-covered field. His black Labrador Retriever then shags the tennis balls as Tom works the driver.

Now *that's* dedication.

For the past couple of years I had been after Tom to play a premium course called Arcadia Bluffs Golf Club, but busy schedules and emergent issues seemed to always get in the way. Finally, the planets aligned and we found a date that worked for both of us. Don Brandt would join us, along with Tom's oldest son Zack, a student down at Western Michigan University.

Arcadia Bluffs sits on a rolling set of hills above Lake Michigan, neatly guarded on the West side by 400-foot cliffs that drop down to a narrow lake shoreline. The views are spectacular from just about every tee box. Born and raised in the Deep South, I had little exposure to the grandeur of the Great Lakes. The concept of a freshwater horizon was foreign to me, but its deep blue contrast to the fairways and elephant grass reminded me of the Carolina ocean courses I grew up cutting my teeth on.

Arcadia Bluffs also sits slap dab in the middle of nowhere, on the Western Coast of Michigan, halfway between Manistee and Frankfort. In fact, it is so remote that the course offers lodging for its guests, because you have to drive like hell just to get back home before the next day's breakfast. So when we set the tee time, all four of us knew it was going to take a strong commitment to play there. Yet, given the course's reputation, we were all eager to make the long drive, knowing it would be well worth every asphalt mile.

Trigger pulled.

When I arrived that morning, Don was already working on his short game—flopping shots onto the chipping green, and blasting shots out of the trap like a mini Ballesteros. Don wasn't going to leave any shots on the course due to lack of preparation. He had no regrets stashed in his bag today.

Side note: a year earlier, Don and I had played The Bluffs, and it was uglier than a bowling shoe. Don scored somewhere short of 90, I shot well over 100, and we both knew it was the layout of the course and the wind whipping off the lake that exposed the weaknesses in our games.

Today we had a second chance, and it would either validate how bad we suck, or erase the previous round from our consciousness.

The Bluffs's roller coaster greens had left quite an impression on me. I could remember one elevated green with a false front and tightly cropped fringe, where Don and I had chipped up above the hole repeatedly—only to have our balls trickle all the way back down the green, and then twenty yards down to our feet to the base of the hill below the green. We hit six chip shots between us, finally reconciling ourselves to leaving our balls in the cut just off of the green and putting from there, en route to one of *many* big numbers that day.

So this morning I practiced putting like I meant it, because I knew my round, and the condition of my wallet, depended on it.

Tom and Zack showed up a little later, and after working out the kinks and loading up provisions (think cold beer and peanuts), we were ready to conquer the course.

• • • •

Though it's inland, Arcadia Bluffs is laid out like a links course, with verdant fairways snaking their way through the amber fescue. Positioned at the same latitude but on the other side of Lake Michigan, the Bluffs carry the same beautiful and daunting characteristics as the more household name Whistling Straits. The flowing fescue is very pretty, unless you're *in* it. It can make even the most confident players reach for an iron off the tee. But we all knew that none of us would play here again anytime soon, so there would be no irons off the box for us.

Grip it, and by God, rip it!

As any golfer worth his salt knows, a round's not near as much fun without a little skin in the game, so a wager betwixt the four of us was *definitely* in order. We settled on a two-man, best ball format, my favorite form of match play, with the very capable Don and me (not quite as capable) taking on Tom and Zack. It was hard to ignore the father-son opportunity, and Don offered it up before I could visualize the benefits of all the other possible options, like playing a scramble, or wild bets like Lewis and Clarks or Reverse Oozlers. No strokes; we'd adjust at the turn if necessary—and, oh yes, gentlemen, play it down.

No rolling, unless it's your ass down a hill after too many Coors Lights.

As it turned out, no adjustment was necessary. The match was tied after nine, with each of us playing to our handicaps and wrestling with the demons the Bluffs had laid out for us. With the exception of a bogey on hole 7, all of the first nine holes were won with a par or better.

At age 21, limber-back Zack had the advantage of scary distance. In many cases, he was able to negate the impact of the hazards that the Bluffs laid before us mere mortals by just pounding it past their reach. But there were enough times where the fickle winds of Lake Michigan caught Zack's ball and tossed it so deep into the high grass that it caused him to double-take his club selection.

Tom's patient game brought balance to their pairing, and father and son were able to ham and egg it for par or better throughout most of the round. As for *our* team, well, I might as well have just put a saddle on Don. Although I was hitting the ball well enough and made a couple of birdies, Don had also made birdie on those same damn holes. You could have called me Sam, as in Samsonite—because I had become luggage.

But Don's many years of practice and studying the game was paying off beautifully, and by the fifteenth tee box we were one hole up on the breakfast club.

Things were looking good.

Number fifteen at the Bluffs is a long, uphill par 5, and by long I mean as long as a bad blind date. The tee box is elevated some 100 feet above the fairway (think 10-story building high), providing ample opportunity for the lake's winds to slap around your golf ball. A bunker for the ages has been well architecturally placed about 230 yards from the tee box, center cut between the elephant grass fairway borders. If the wind is in your favor, you can fly the bunker with no issues. If it's not, you find yourself in a 20-foot wide, 10-foot deep pot bunker bordered by railroad ties.

During our previous round at the Bluffs, Don watched me attempt five shots to get out of said bunker, before taking a drop into the fairway, illegal drop be damned. Solid 9, on that hole—just missed a Bo Derek by one, so I got that going for me.

I asked Don to *please* never speak of it to anyone. He smiled and said, "Speak of what?"

But that was in the past, and as I let bygones be bygones, this time I crushed my drive over the right corner of that dreaded pot bunker, carried by the wind and landing safely in the fairway. Don was not so lucky; his shot caught the top lip of that beastly bunker and kicked backwards into it, coming to rest at the base of a railroad tie. He wisely lofted a sand wedge *backwards* 10 yards into the fairway.

Best to learn from history than to repeat it.

Don's pot bunker issue, my piss-poor putting on fifteen, and two more pushed holes put us right back at even with the father-son duo going into eighteen. Suddenly, the conversation turned crickets-chirping quiet.

Did someone just die?

It had been a great day, we appreciated the company, and we had overcome a lot of challenges just to get here and compete on such a special track, but things had just gotten awkwardly serious.

To each of us, the proposition was clear: the quickest way to toss water on this great day on the links was . . . to lose. And there was just one more hole to play to make the day perfect, a day of golf for the ages.

The 18th hole at Arcadia Bluffs. Butt cheeks tighter than Dick's hatband, hands shaking like a car out of line on both front wheels. Man, is this great golf or what!

All four tee shots split the tight eighteenth fairway for the first time all day. Tom and Zack then both placed their approach shots on the dance floor. Nice. Not to be left out of the party, I also put my ball on the green—check me out. Looking to break 80 with a par, Don decided to shoot for the widest part of the green. Unfortunately,

The 18th green at The Bluffs, with an authentic bagpiper playing "Amazing Grace" as the sun sets over Lake Michigan, giving storyteller Tim Gaffney chills he still feels to this day. Good chills. (*Photo by Adam Ikamas*)

Mother Nature felt there was only room for three on the green and her winds pushed his ball into the deep spinach, just to the right of the green.

It's not nice to mess with Mother Nature.

After his missed green debacle, Don deftly chipped up to 2 feet for a gimmie par. Tom, Zack, and I all were laying two, each of us trying to visualize the line for our birdie putts, all nervous as a preacher with no sermon and the pulpit calling our name.

I was farthest out, with a 20-foot downhill putt. Out of respect for the greens-keeper, I gently tapped the ball to get it moving. It built up speed, burned the upper edge of the cup, and came to rest one foot behind the hole. Tom conceded the putt, and I thanked him. God bless you, Tom. Not sure I could have marked that biscuit and canned it some 2 minutes later.

Zack's putt was up next, 15 feet uphill, no break, just meat and potatoes.

Zack drained it for birdie. Great putt under the gun but damn, damn, damn!

Tom's ball sat 12 feet from the cup on a knoll that created a sharp left to right downhill line. He almost had to putt sideways to get it rolling, but the ball seemed to be sucked down into the hole: birdie. Our foursome erupted—high fives all around, and Tom hugged his son in victory. At that exact moment, I looked to my right and saw that a bagpiper had ascended the hill above the green and began playing his pipes. I don't recall the tune, *Amazing Grace* maybe?

But I completely remember its effect on me.

I still get chills.

After that spiritual round at the Bluffs, we had an incredible dinner at the clubhouse and recapped the great moments from the day. Although no one would say it, we all knew that this was a round that was different, special.

Don and I had each redeemed ourselves—we could put the previous Arcadia Bluffs round behind us. And my dear friend Tom had just spent an unforgettable day with his son whom he loves dearly, on perhaps the finest golf course in Michigan—or even America.

After my friends left, I stayed behind to reflect upon the day and take in the fading rainbow-colored sunset over Lake Michigan, a vista you absolutely need to put on your bucket list. A couple rows of white lawn chairs had been positioned overlooking the Lake to accommodate my interest. It worked.

Knee deep in fescue, the bagpiper was still playing tunes for other guests as they enjoyed cocktails on the Bluffs . . . unforgettable.

I pray I get a chance to remember it again.

Chapter 4

MAKALIA GOLF CLUB

Kailua-Kona, Hawaii

7,091 yards

By Judson Hill, the small-town boy who made good

This curious adventure begins with benign intentions.

Imagine two best friends, fresh out of law school, flying the friendly skies with the Hawaiian Islands as our final destination. I'm 26, newly married, the gold band on my hand still shining as bright as the diamond on my lovely wife's, just starting my law career and trying to find my way. I know just enough to know I don't know anything, except a great deal when I see one.

Or in this case, hear one.

My office phone rings and it's my best friend Brian Cahn. We've been best buds since high school, when we were arrested and booked for trying to buy beer at a Quickie Mart the very first night we hung out together. We even made the hometown newspaper, albeit not the front page. How's *that* for an introduction to a lifelong friendship?

With AT&T's finest cradled against my ear, I hear the wildly excited voice of said best friend Brian, who has sniffed out round-trip airfare from Atlanta to Honolulu for just $178 each. Brian is a bloodhound when it comes to sniffing out good deals. We are young, money is tighter than chiggers on tube socks, but at that price we are in.

By God, are we ever in!

For those who like a good visual, Brian is just shy of 6 feet, clocking in at 190 rock solid pounds, handsome, and smooth as a Velvet Elvis with the ladies. I'm built more like the Scarecrow from *The Wizard of Oz*. (Great movie, by the way; hold the straw, please. I too am somewhat smooth with the ladies, but when I found the right one, I changed that noun from plural to singular.)

Maybe that's why Brian and I are best friends. We couldn't look more different, and oftentimes act more different, but our hearts are one and the same. And we both love the game of golf like we're something out of the psych ward!

Once hearing the sweet plane ticket news, I tell Brian that an older lawyer friend of mine has a house on the Big Island, albeit on the side of a volcano (not sure if it's active or not; let's hope not) though smack dab in the middle of a rain forest. My old friend graciously offers up his basement apartment to us gratis. Free is good, very good, especially when your wallet has more lint in it than Benjamins. To cut costs like a do-it-yourself junkie, we plan on staying there the first 3 nights.

Maybe longer, if we can get away with it.

From the outset, I tell Brian we gotta, just gotta play Mauna Kea, the celebrated Hawaiian Islands track that is the talk of *Golf Digest's Top 50 Greatest Golf Courses in America*. It's only one of the coolest courses in the world, and it's right where we're going for goodness sake, this magical place where we will likely never return.

Sadly, Brian is not having any part of my grand idea. This man is NOT going to spend that kind of dough to hit a golf ball, Hawaiian Islands be damned.

After weeks of lobbying for the cause, I finally abandon plans for the unattainable $290 (yes, *more* than our 4,500-mile round-trip plane flight) dream round at Mauna Kea. Brian simply isn't going to do it. To his credit, he has sniffed out an alternative: Makalei Golf Club. Info on the Makalei Golf Club is scarce, like trying to find a gold necklace on the beach, and you without a metal detector and scoop bucket, but Brian has confirmed that Makalei is far more wallet-friendly than Mauna Kea.

He would know, so off we go into the clouds. Let the games begin!

After a night of Hawaiian festivities, food and beverages, and some things I will take to the grave, I wake up still a bit salty about the turn of events, and a bit, make that a big bit (like the one in the mouth of Secretariat), hung over as hell.

But that's no hill for a climber like me.

With high hopes, Brian and I trek up a long and winding mountain road in a tuna fish gray Pontiac Grand Le Mans with lots of miles and vinyl seats slicker than a used car salesman. But she's chugging along just fine, hairpin turn after hairpin turn; hairpin turns so tight I feel like we're turning around backwards. After what seems like forever (and with my life flashing before me!), we come around yet another hairpin turn and there she is: the grand Makalei Golf Club.

I can't believe how beautiful the vistas are. To our left, we see whales surfacing in the Pacific—*real* whales, like the kind you pay big money to charter a boat and have a sighting kind. On the vast horizon we see the Mauna Kea volcano, bordered by the nickel-blue water of the Kohala Coast, waves crashing with bouncing silver streaks, stretching far as the eye can see. Directly in front of us are huge, and I mean ostrich huge, Crayola-colored peacocks with their feathers unfurled, meandering along the property without a care in the world. I can't help but wonder: How the hell did they get here? They can hardly fly from the hood of this Pontiac to the trunk!

Also, to our meandering right, the Makalei golf course stretches up down and around a mountain whose name escapes me. My mood is improving. Anticipation replaces aggravation, and after a quick and affordable green fee paid in the pro shop (a very manageable 25 bucks), it's off to the first tee.

Peg in, ball up, game on.

The first hole at Makalei is a par 4, straight up the mountain, but a mere 311 yards. Driver, sand wedge, if that. In spite of my physical condition from the night of Hawaiian festivities, I absolutely stripe my drive; it flies 245 into the crisp Hawaiian air, and I'm posing on that first tee shot like a Victoria Secret supermodel on runway night. My brand spanking new Titleist lands and bounds forward hard, cement hard, and now I'm thinking 275, maybe even 280, but then it stops suddenly, like it's made out of lead, not balata. Then it commences a slow but steady roll back down the mountain.

The Pacific Ocean offers breathtaking vistas to golfers on the Big Island. I think I see my Titleist 3 down there amongst the rocks. (*ejs9, courtesy of iStock*)

Like *way* back.

After what seems like 5 minutes, my Titleist golf ball comes to a stop roughly 20 yards from the front of the tee box, where I am standing, and now Brian and I are laughing our asses off.

How could we not?

And so it goes for 18 holes. Each hole at Makalei seems flawed in insurmountable ways, be it condition, design, or simply karma. All day long we hit 90-yard drives up the mountain, 300-yard 7-irons down it, onto fairways dry as your uncle's favorite and oft-repeated joke. Well-played iron shots into the green (granted, there were few) bounced like one of those gumball machine rock-hard rubber super-balls you played with when you were a kid. There are wild goats for days, eating shrubbery and grass, and pooping. And all the while we are riding in an old school Yamaha gas cart with a serious governor. Going up the mountain is so slow my Great Aunt Lucille (at this time aged 86) could have skipped circles around us like a frisky sherpa!

Mauna Kea, it was not.

Yet, in spite of all this, I still rate Makalei as my greatest golf experience ever. The beer and laughs flowed all round long with my best friend for life, in a place that life will never take us back to. It was bad golf on a bizarre track, surrounded by the most incredibly beautiful scenery I have ever witnessed, before or since. Simply put, it was something else.

You talk about all the memorable rounds? Well, this was mine. Truly a memory for the nursing home, if and when I get there.

I don't want to rush it.

• • • •

Author's Note: Though Judson told me this story a year and a half after an article on the recent changes at Makalei was written by Jason Scott Deegan, a golf advisor and blogger, I find it rather prophetic Judson's depiction of the first hole at Makalei and his memorable experience soon followed. Judson had not seen the article until *after* he shared his classic golf story with me, which makes it all the more prophetic.

The long and the short of Jason's well-written article is that the starting hole at Makalei Golf Club is now the old number 8 and much closer to the practice tee, which used to be over a 500-yard drive from the pro shop—how is that for one heck of a trek—over mountainous volcanic terrain, dodging those cart-path-hugging peacocks. Word on the Hawaiian street says the opening hole is much flatter, too, so you don't have to worry about starting off your bargain yet memorable round of golf in the Hawaiian Islands with your first tee shot rolling back to the toes of your shoes!

I can't help but wonder if the ghost of our Aunt Lucille is still skipping like a frisky sherpa around the grounds of Makalei, or perhaps she is simply enjoying a vodka tonic with a squeeze of lime on the veranda, overlooking an active volcano. The vodka tonic—Aunt Lucille's favorite 5 o'clock beverage.

Time will tell.

Chapter 5

SHADY OAKS
COUNTRY CLUB

Fort Worth, Texas

6,919 yards

By Dave Cearley, Associate Professor
of Pediatric Orthopedic Surgery at Augusta
University, and the kid from the trailer park

Growing up in Fort Worth, Texas, I thought Colonial Country Club was the end all be all of golf courses, the pinnacle, because it was the one everybody always talked about, the one that held the celebrated Colonial PGA Tour event, the course always so closely associated with Ben Hogan, who, along with Byron Nelson, were Fort Worth's favorite native sons. But as I got older and learned more about golf, I learned that Ben Hogan was actually spending his days at Shady Oaks, not Colonial Country Club, that he considered Shady Oaks his home course, and that he had even helped to build and design the course—even though you don't see much about that in the history books.

I certainly didn't know it.

Being an avid golf fan and lover of the game, although I wasn't a student of the game (I wasn't a very good player at the time), I chose Shady Oaks as the place I wanted to hang out during the summer of my 23rd year, the summer before my second year of med school at Texas A&M. All my friends were getting jobs in labs, learning more about blood and guts, but I wanted to get sweaty, and learn about the earth and the sky, and soak up as much Texas heat and all that I could about the game of golf. And Shady Oaks was the place to do it.

Not being wealthy enough to join the club, I took a job there, first bussing tables and then later in the golf shop, clocking in at 7 a.m., getting the carts ready with the right clubs on the right carts at the right time, because I quickly learned who the early birds were, and they appeared like clockwork. Cleaning clubs, helping organize for tournaments, shagging balls, whatever they asked me to do, I did. Lunch break was: "Have you eaten yet?" I would say no, and they'd tell me to haul my ass to the kitchen, see what was left, and haul my ass right back.

Growing up a poor kid in Texas (my dad died young, and my mom was a school teacher), I didn't really know what to expect about Country Clubbers, but the people there were really nice, from the staff to the membership; it was one of the nicest places I've ever been a part of. Everybody was respectful to each other, to me, and there were a lot of good tippers, which was good because I needed every nickel I could get.

Nobody was overly demanding, and nobody was condescending. I always felt very privileged to be there, to get a glimpse into a world I never thought I would ever see.

Because I was a little older than the rest of the guys, I garnered some of the favor of the assistant pros. They could tell I was really there to learn about the game of golf and not just shag balls or park carts to earn a buck. So they started teaching me a little bit, giving me pointers here and there, and ultimately letting me play the course with them. Once I showed them I had a respect and knowledge for the game and how it was truly meant to be played, they let me play the course by myself. I didn't appreciate the true quality of the course at the time; I was just happy to be playing such a nice course for free, getting advice and tips from the assistant pros, advice I later learned were lessons from Ben Hogan himself, who had hand-picked these guys to be his teaching pros, at *his* course. What a fool I was. Getting golf lessons from pros hand-picked by Mr. Hogan and I didn't even know it. But it was a good time to be a fool in my life. After all, I was only 23.

Shady Oaks was truly Mr. Hogan's course.

Everything about that place reflected Mr. Hogan's values, his respect for the game, and his love of the game. Everyone there referred to him as Mr. Hogan—I can't recall anyone ever calling him Ben, except maybe his wife. At that time he was still showing up and holding court at his table overlooking the 18th green. Though he was starting to get old and frail and falling off a bit, he would still come out to the course every day, from about noon to 4 o'clock, where he would see the main group go off and come back, and they would come in, pay their respects, and he would give them pointers. Then he would leave and head for the house.

But the pros at Shady Oaks, their teaching, revolved around Hogan's Way. No one knows for sure what Hogan's Way was—nothing was ever written down, but for me, two things come to mind. The first is what Mr. Hogan always did until he got too old and frail to do it anymore—and that is practice. There is no substitute for practice, no substitute for digging it out of the dirt. But the one thing his pros kept telling me, and the one thing I kept hearing them tell the members when they'd give them lessons, and this may sound a little crazy, was keeping the flex in the right knee constant throughout the swing. Never allow that right leg to move during the backswing. Also, starting the swing with a forward press with the right leg toward the target, then locking that in place, and keeping that stable, as a pivot point around which to turn—when you do that, *if* you can do that, the accuracy and consistency of your shots is phenomenally

It's been said that the great Jack Nicklaus would often watch The Wee Ice Mon practice, though The Wee Ice Mon never *once* watched Nicklaus practice. (*AP Photo*)

better than when you allow yourself to sway back and forth. Not to mention the fact that you get about ten yards more of distance this way.

It's impossible to hit it fat, impossible to hit it thin, if you keep the right leg stable. The flex in the right knee is what generates the power and the accuracy and consistency of the swing. If you look at old school swing sequence photos of Hogan's swing, that is the one thing he did better than anybody else.

But it wasn't until some years later, when I moved to Augusta to practice medicine, that I would come to realize why Hogan chose Shady Oaks over Colonial to call home. While in Augusta, I was fortunate to attend the Masters, even play the National, and when I flew back home to play Shady Oaks for the first time as a guest and not a cart boy with some of my old fraternity brothers, I realized why Hogan did what he did, why he spent his time there, and not at Colonial.

Because Shady Oaks was the Hogan *he* knew, not the Hogan people thought *they* knew.

Colonial is a shot-makers course, sure, but it's flat—built along a riverbed. Shady Oaks is built on a hill. It starts low and works its way up high and then back down again. It's the highest point in Fort Worth, and just a few miles from where Hogan grew up. Given these facts, there was no doubt in my mind that day after walking off the 18th green at Shady Oaks, having played Augusta National just a few weeks before, why Hogan built his course there. Not only is it on a hill, but it has elevation changes just like the National, though in reverse. The National starts high and works low and comes back up. But in between there's lots of hills, lots of slopes, and tons of elevation changes. Hogan also uses plenty of doglegs, just like Augusta National, but the most striking thing about it, for that area, are the elevation changes. Apparently, that sort of terrain creates slopes on the greens that you can't see, ghost slopes—just like at Augusta.

There's no doubt in my mind that Hogan chose and agreed to that specific piece of property, Amon G. Carter's old ranch, to build his own Augusta National, even though the Shady Oaks website says just the opposite. Yes, Mr. Hogan's trophies are at Colonial. Yes, Mr. Hogan's statue is at Colonial. But his heart is at Shady Oaks.

Mine, too.

Chapter 6

AUGUSTA NATIONAL GOLF CLUB (PART I)

Augusta, Georgia

6,980 yards

By Tripp Bowden

My perspective of playing Augusta National is oddly unique, in that it is threefold.

I came in as a free-wheeling ten-year-old kid just learning the game, as a 21-year-old Augusta National caddy—the *only* white boy in the bunch—and then as a married man with a mortgage and an SUV, just like country singer Mark Willis describes it in the song *19 Somethin'*.

Life-defining lyrics, if you grew up in the seventies and eighties like I did.

My first *memory* of Augusta National is a simple photograph. It was part of a slide show (remember slides?) my doctor dad often used for a talk he put together and one that he often changed and exchanged (except for this photograph) for his annual presentation to the Georgia Surgical Society.

I was ten years old at the time, and knew as much about golf as I did about surgery.

In the shades-down-dark of my dad's upstairs office, his slide presentation carousel whirled and stopped on a breathtaking wintertime photo of Augusta's treacherous 12th, the unforgiving par 3 with always swirling winds challenging a 155-yard carry over Rae's Creek. Everything in this photograph is white from a rare southern snowfall. Everything, from the tall loblolly pines to the banks of Rae's Creek, is eggshell white except for the green, which I quickly learned is heated and cooled year round by a clever contraption hidden in a pump house left of the greenside pond on number 11.

The 12th green at Augusta is a balmy 72 degrees all year long.

How cool is *that*?

After hanging onto my dad's every word about the mystery of the 12th, I—the punk kid who had yet to break 100 and didn't make his 8th grade golf team (just like Michael Jordan didn't make his basketball team in same said grade, but that's where the comparison ends)—would soon play Augusta National many times as a guest of the pro's son, during what was known as Closing Week. Closing Week: seven days of tee times every seven minutes, when tournament big wigs and even the not so big wigs, scorekeepers, grounds crew, staff, and the caddies got their chance to put a peg in the ground and experience Augusta during the helpers-outers hallowed third week in May.

Mr. Clifford Roberts, founder of Augusta National along with Bobby Jones, always made sure that was a nice enough thank you for your services.

Man, was it ever.

• • • •

My first *impression* of Augusta's hallowed Augusta grounds?

How lush yet flat to the ground the grass was, as if the grass preferred to grow sideways but not up, and so soft, even with shoes on, like walking on a big, green Willie Wonka cloud. As if I could just reach out and grab an Everlasting Gobstopper or a Fizzy Lifting Drink.

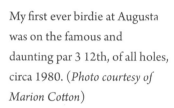

My first ever birdie at Augusta was on the famous and daunting par 3 12th, of all holes, circa 1980. (*Photo courtesy of Marion Cotton*)

Then there were the tee boxes at Augusta, which were easily as fast as most greens I had ever played (I do remember putting on them, just to satisfy my curiosity), with the air around them wafting of tradition and reverence, and the grounds so quiet, so incredibly quiet. All those people milling about, and I don't remember hearing a single voice raised above a whisper.

Fast forward ten years later, and I'm a college graduate and the proud owner of a degree in English with minors in philosophy and psychology (let me know if you would like to buy one—I am selling them on the cheap). Those degrees and minors make for a lot of fun if you want to be a writer, but they don't always pay the bills. Truth be told, right now I'm as lost as a preacher with no sermon, with the congregation filing in fast. I'm either going to teach, drink beer all summer, or stare out windows.

For the record, I did the latter two. Quite well, I might add.

But luck shined on me once again when Freddie Bennett, Augusta's legendary Caddy Master and a very dear friend of my father's, took me under his wing for the second time in my young life and gave me a job. I was the first full-time white caddy at Augusta National, with a backstage pass to the hallowed club, thanks to Freddie. Access to all areas. I felt like the luckiest man alive.

Looking back, I believe I was.

I learned so much as an Augusta National caddy, though very little on my own. I was fortunate enough to have many teachers, every one of them with their own special insight into the brotherhood of caddying. There are too many to list here, but let me tell you a story that involves one of my favorites.

His name was Sydney Brown, and as I recall the words, this is what he preached to me in his rapid fire delivery: "You don't read Augusta greens, my man; you *remember* them."

Sydney learned that from Freddie, and Sydney paid it forward to me.

I will never forget the day Sydney casually snatched the putter out of an unsuspecting player's hands who was reading his putt Ben Crenshaw-style, right hand on the grip, left hand on the blade, holding it out in front of him like a treasure map.

Me playing the Nash during Closing Week, Circa 1988. I'm in a no-topper cart trying to play as many holes as possible on that Friday in May, not knowing if I may ever get the chance to play these hallowed grounds again. (*Photo courtesy of Marion Cotton*)

"Ain't no plumb bobbin' out here, no sir," said Sydney, his player's putter raised to the sky as if in effigy. "Oh, hell naw. Not in my group. Now go'ne an' put that plumb bob back in ya' bag, and don't lemme see it again or I'm a'gonna whoop ya' eight ways to Sunday!"

Sydney didn't give back that goofy-looking Ping putter until the player promised to *never* plumb bob at Augusta, for as long as he lived, so help him God. For the record, that player was a *member*, CEO of a Fortune 500 Company, and Sydney was and still is, though posthumously as they both have passed (so I'm told), the *only* caddy this member ever had.

A beautiful testament to how much Sydney meant to his main man, and his main man to him.

To this day, whenever I'm watching the Masters (this year, 2017, will be my 40th in a row), the moment a Titleist or Calloway or whatever brand of golf ball starts rolling across those greens I say to myself, "Well remembered, or no chance in hell." I can still read 'em, even from outside the ropes. Those greens haven't changed.

Their memory is the same as mine.

And it's the same as that of the legendary Augusta caddy Mark Eubanks, who was burly as Babe the Ox with a voice like gravel, and toted well the rock for Hall Of Famer Johnny Miller back in the day, en route to *three* runner-up finishes—1971, '75, and '81. Mark once said to me, as we were walking up the hill on number 5, after I had missed the absolute living shit out of a *read* and not a *remembrance*: "White Boy, the ball's gonna *do* what the ball's gonna *do*!"

I learned the hard way, Mark, but I did ultimately learn. Thank you for sharing your wisdom with me.

• • • •

As caddies, we were allowed to play Augusta just once a year, the final day of Closing Week, when folks who help out with the Masters (think scorekeepers, security, et al.) and club employees get to play golf till they drop and/or fish the par 3 course for bream and bass. Don't try to catch a carp (there's a kids song about doing something similar), as they only eat algae. Augusta's carp are big, as in golf bag big, and could feed a family

My Augusta National caddy ID badge. Me, the first ever full-time white caddy at Augusta National. How wild is that? (*Photo courtesy of Freddie Bennett*)

of 10 with leftovers for the neighbors if they dig fish, but carp are vegetarians; they care not for what is on your hook if it is worm or minnow. Only way you are catching one of those mothers is if you dive into Ike's Pond and wrestle one to the shore.

Good luck with that.

Fishing talk aside, there is truly *nothing* in the golfing world like Caddy Day at Augusta National Golf Club.

Except for the clubhouse, we caddies had free run of those hallowed grounds, and I mean free like kids on a playground with the school long closed. Tee off at sunrise, and by sunrise I mean you can barely see the first tee box, much less the green in the distance, with four carts in your foursome as you try to break the record for most holes played in one day—105, if memory serves—I held it for quite some time. Fish Ike's Pond with your new friends, fellow caddies who taught you to love the looping side of the game as much as the game itself. Sit on the veranda just like a dues-paying member, drinking cold keg beer and smoking Kool Menthol cigarettes while telling funny-ass stories about guests playing Augusta for the very first time, such as—"Som'bitch asked me for a read on number one and I said, 'Soon as your knees stop shaking, knock it s'craight in the cup!'"

I could go on and on. Perhaps, one day, I will.

Strange as it may sound, the golf seemed almost secondary. Imagine finally getting to talk to a beautiful woman who you only know because she walks by your cubicle every day and sometimes smiles at you. On Caddy Day, you get to learn that beautiful woman's name, her likes and dislikes, her hopes and dreams, her thoughts and wishes. And she gets to learn yours. And if only for that day, she belongs to you.

• • • •

Fast forward another ten years and see me sitting in a salon chair getting a haircut. My phone rings, and normally I would hit the "no thanks, I'm busy" button, but I see it's my dad and I answer. Pop rarely dials my digits, so it must be important. I put the phone to my ear.

"Hey, Smoke! Want to play Augusta tomorrow?"

I drop my jaw, and then my phone.

I have never played Augusta as the guest of a member, and truly never thought I would. I'm having trouble catching my breath. My hair stylist, though there is nothing really to style, with my surfer dude blonde locks thin as angel hair spaghetti and straight as a wooden fence, thinks surely there has been a death in the family, and her eyes well with tears. She has never seen me this full of silence.

Funny, neither have I, before or since.

Less than 24 hours and a short two-hour drive from our home in Atlanta later, I'm gliding through the front gate at Augusta with my dad, and straight down Magnolia Lane. No sharp right turn to the Caddy Barn. No gravel parking lot for me, baby! Not today.

A quick shoe change and tour of the clubhouse later (how cool it was to see and touch Bobby Jones's locker), and wow! I'm suddenly on the west practice tee at Augusta, ready but not, to start my once in a lifetime day. I gotta admit it feels a little odd to be on the other side of the white jumpsuit that had been my clothing of choice for four straight years of my roller coaster life, especially when I am greeted by my caddy, who

Seriously?

My caddie looks at me blank as a preschool canvas and in all seriousness says, with my golf clubs hanging on his shoulder like bats in a cave, "Uh, now what?"

I'll let you take a guess at what my answer was. Let's just say God has a wonderful sense of humor, and, lucky for my green as grapes caddy, so do I.

By day's end, I end up teaching that kid more about caddying at Augusta National in four short hours than he could ever learn in a lifetime of just smashing grass. Time flies when you're having fun, kid!

Ain't no doubt, a lot of water has washed under the bridge since that day, and my life is very different and so are my perspectives. As for my perspective of playing Augusta National as the guest of a card-carrying member? I hope this won't jeopardize my chances of ever getting invited back, but I gotta be honest.

There ain't *nothing* quite like Caddy Day.

Chapter 7

PINEHURST RESORT, PINEHURST NO. 2

Pinehurst, North Carolina

7,565 yards

By Trey Holroyd, the kid whose life was forever changed by Putter Boy

I'll do my best to set the stage, greenhorn storyteller that I am.

It's a Friday, 1986, summertime in the South, and I'm with my best bud William Lanier, with high school in our rearview mirror. I've just welcomed Ernie Lanford, the head golf coach at local Augusta College, into the den of my parents' house, only to tell Coach Lanford that as much as I appreciated his full ride scholarship offer, I was going to be looking elsewhere.

I just felt like I had to leave Augusta if I was ever going to be the caliber of golfer I dreamed of being.

Those were hard words to say to Ernie—one of the nicest folks you'll ever meet. Even though Augusta College played Division I in golf (Division II in the other sports), it just, at least in the year 1986, wasn't nearly big enough for me. I was bound and determined to play Division I golf for a *big time* school. I dreamt of a school that had a football team with cheerleaders and all the Saturday high noon electricity that goes with game day college football, a school offering much more than just a good chance to play for the NCAA Championship, but a chance to win it all. At the time, Augusta had never even ever *been* to the NCAA Championship in golf, much less won it, though some 20 years later they would go out and do just that, not just once but twice!

I won't lie. I wanted bright lights, big city, like my best buddy Wally Burger, who had signed a ticket to ride with powerhouse LSU. I felt with all the hours I'd put in, I deserved at least a *chance* at the big ticket.

But at the moment, I had nothing—no offers whatsoever from the big boys, in spite of what I thought was a pretty decent junior golf career. I had even recently won a high school state championship, the Tar Heel Junior Open, the Augusta City Junior Amateur, and a slot in the U.S. Junior Amateur, after being medalist in the state qualifier.

Pretty scary, looking back on it, me with my high school diploma in one hand, my 5-time refinished Toney Penna persimmon driver in the other, and absolutely no clue where I was going to college, to play golf, and chase my dream. I felt kind of strange turning down a scholarship offer from Coach Lanford seeing as I had none on the table—"stupid" might be the better word—but in my heart I really felt I had to go away from home to find my game, to find myself.

Lying on my bed and staring at the ceiling fan spinning round and round, I started reflecting back to the summer before, when I spent a solid week with my brother June Bug and a couple other kids, Chip Ivey and Will Darnell, I think it was, on the Georgia coast. During that time, we were learning from the legendary Davis Love Sr., one of the greatest teachers the game has ever known, and even stayed at his house in St. Simons, Georgia. I got to meet his son, eventual PGA Tour professional and Major Championship winner Davis Love III, who at the time was attending UNC in Chapel Hill, starring on their golf team and hanging out with Michael Jordan.

Seeing that Putter Boy trophy perched on the mantle at Davis's house—Davis had recently won the prestigious Pinehurst North & South Amateur Championship, one of the premier amateur golf tournaments in the world—I knew I had to have one. I knew that Putter Boy, the most iconic image in all of American golf, would validate me, get me the big-time college scholarship offers I thought I was worthy of. Or at least get me *one*, and that was all I needed.

Just like a bunch of the kids I grew up playing golf with out at West Lake Country Club (think laid back and blue collar), I put in countless hours practicing, playing, grinding, and sweating profusely under a relentless Southern sun, never missing a day. I had worked to be the absolute best I could be, and yet here I was with zero offers to play college golf at the highest level.

Putter Boy could change all that. So I set out to go get him.

After a restless night of sleep in that bedroom with the ceiling fan spinning mindlessly, I woke the next morning with a promise to stop feeling so dang sorry for myself, and virtually willed myself to have the best tournament summer of any junior golfer in the country. Yes, that's a lot to ask of myself seeing as I had never really traveled to any of the so-called watermark AJGA tourneys, mostly because of the locations and travel costs, so my victories were local for the most part, which was likely why I wasn't on anyone's radar but that of Augusta College. But I knew that the North & South Junior Championship, if I could somehow work magic and pull out a W, would take me to the next level and get me on the Doppler radar of big-time college golf.

• • • •

The road leading to Pinehurst from Augusta begins on Interstate 20, then it's Highway 1 and backroads the rest of the way, with not a lot to see but towering pine trees and sand until you get to one of the hidden golf capitals of the world, Southern Pines, North Carolina, peppered with phenomenal golf courses far as the eye can see. And then there's the granddaddy of them all: Pinehurst No. 2, by far and away the most untouchable golf course I will ever have the chance of playing in my young golf career. To step out onto such hallowed grounds, to feel my FootJoy tungsten spikes sink into

First Light at Pinehurst. (*Photo by Pinehurst Resort grounds crew greens guru Kaye Pierson*)

the soft, rich earth, and think of all the legendary golfers who'd come before me and made their mark there, it literally took my breath away.

I'd never seen a golf course like this before, and I'd been around the game literally all my life, hitting plastic golf balls with an equally plastic club as soon as I could walk. The product, if that's even the right word, was absolute perfection, from tee to green to the shrubs to the smiling faces in the pro shop. From hitting range balls on the exquisitely manicured practice tee with the ball sitting up perfectly on groomed Bermuda turf, to rolling putts on a green so smooth and slick I can't help but rub my fingers on the bent grass to make sure it's real. The Pinehurst No. 2 experience is so magically surreal I don't ever want to leave. But leave I do. Have to.

The sun has set and it's so dark I can't see the tip of my nose, which is a pretty big target.

Soon I'm sitting in our hotel room, a Days Inn just down the road, channeling best I can the great Jack Nicklaus from his classic instruction book *Golf My Way*, with my mom snoozing serenely in the queen-sized bed beside me, and me visually playing the holes of Pinehurst No. 2 in my mind, 1-18, over and over and over again. Where not to hit it, where do you *want* to hit it? What score would be a good number here, there? When to play safe, when to throw caution to the wind and over those miles of natural bunkers and weeping lovegrass? If I could get through the first 5 holes even par—with the par 4 5th being harder than the par 5 4th, I just might have a chance to make some noise.

Before I know it, the sun, creeping up and now over the horizon, arrives like a surprise, and though I haven't slept much (did I even sleep at all?), I feel great. A new day has dawned, a new me has dawned, and I pray I am ready for both. Putter Boy tells me maybe, just maybe I am. He talks to me, you know, with his squeaky, little high-pitched voice. Though he doesn't move his lips much and won't look me in the eye.

C'mon, I'm kidding. Just wanted to see if you were still paying attention.

• • • •

The North & South Junior Championship is a three-day, medal play event, and I must admit the first couple days are an absolute electric blur, in spite of my still youthful 16-year-old mind. In spite of shooting a right-there-in-the-mix 75 and 74 in rounds one and two, all I can collectively recall are rain delays, sand for days, and gargantuan loblolly pines lining the fairways. I do remember my mom being there on this particular occasion—I was fortunate enough to have one or both of my parents travel with me more often than not, my mom especially, as my dad was often holding down the fort at his architectural firm to keep the lights on, and in this case he was. I find myself feeding off the difficult to describe energy that is family that loves you, believes in you. I cherish having my folks with me when I play in tournaments, be it Mom or Dad or both.

But like I said, I don't remember a whole lot about days 1 and 2, except having my mom walk the course with me, taking every step I take, smiling her wonderful smile, and Dad leaving the pep talks back at home.

Anyone who knows me knows that I simply don't like pep talks. Save that for *Barney*; it's gonna fall on deaf ears with me. Please don't ever give me a pep talk, which is very hard for my dad (or any dad for that matter) to do when they see their kid struggling. I know what I know; I know what I see; I know what I am up against. Please let me handle it best I know how.

And that third and final day, how to describe it? It is just a really beautiful moment in time in that I am simply just playing the game of golf, albeit for one heck of a lifetime prize, doing what I always felt I was put on this earth to do, with Mom watching and Dad watching from a distance, both being supportive without words. For reasons I'm not sure I'm capable of explaining, I don't feel the pressure to have to prove myself like in so many other tournaments before.

I know this may sound odd, but Putter Boy is driving me. I can't help it, can't get that iconic trophy out of my mind, seeing it sitting there on the mantle of future PGA Champion Davis Love III's house as real as rain, and now the very real possibility of it sitting on mine. It could serve as validation for all the hard work, the daily grinding, and the labor of love I had put in since first picking up a club.

Trust it, T. Play with confidence, stay the course. Come on man, you got this!

On the par 5 16th, I get a very, and I mean very good break. I hit a nasty bow-wang off the box, high and sweeping hard left and headed for doom, but luck is with me (I would much rather be lucky than good) and my tee shot rattles off the pines and back into the fairway. I wedge it onto the green, two-putt for par, and move on. I also manage to par the tricky 17th, in spite of hitting it long and left off the tee. I hit maybe the shot of the day for me, a really sweet pitch that nestles gimmie-close to the flagstick—guaranteed makeable, even with hands shaking like a blender.

And then, standing on the 18th tee at Pinehurst No. 2 with the North & South Junior Championship mine for the taking, I'm told I have a two-shot lead, after starting the day one shot back. A two-shot lead! I had no idea. All I gotta do is par or even bogey this hole and I win. And look at that beautiful, rolling green fairway, just waiting for a striped drive down the middle.

Putter Boy is just 5 shots away!

I tee up my Titleist and settle into my stance, feet square and shoulders slightly open to ensure a fade, waggle twice, and promptly snatch that biscuit dead left into the weeping lovegrass—the dreaded lovegrass, where there is no love whatsoever unless your idea of love is a double bogey. But when I get to my ball, chin dragging the ground, admittedly, I see I have a decent lie and by decent I mean I can at least *see* the top of the ball. It's not the best lie by any stretch, but at least it offers a chance to get my Titleist 384 the hell out of there and back onto the fairway. My dad is there, waiting on me, and without words (because he is there in spirit, not flesh) I hear him say, "Hang in there, Trey. Hang in there, son, play smart. You're ok."

So I take wedge instead of a 6-iron like the old me would have done, and hit out of that loveless grass as hard as my 16-year-old body will let me, and when my ball bounds back out into the middle of the fairway, I start breathing again.

Not a thing of beauty, but still a joy forever.

I manage to sneak my third shot onto the green and I'm thinking: all I gotta do is make bogey. Just two-putt, man, all you gotta do is two-putt. That's not an easy thing to do when your heart is in your throat, and you're leaking oil like the Valdez.

When I get to the very crowned 18th green (this is a Donald Ross design, so of course they are crowned like the Queen of England!), I see I've got a thirty-footer, just a touch uphill. But with my brain not even thinking about grain I leave it 5 feet short. Five feet short! A five-footer stands between me and Putter Boy and everything I've dreamed of.

I'm not sure who drained the next one. Was it God? The ghost of Bobby Jones? But I do know this: it damned sure wasn't me.

Best bogey of my life.

A partial ride golf scholarship to the mighty Georgia Institute of Technology quickly followed (yes, the good ol' MIT of the South, a place I could have *never* gotten into academically and not entirely sure how I got *out* of) and four years later I was on my way.

Putter Boy is finally home. How about that, game of golf? Never give up on your dreams, y'all! Chase 'em and catch 'em! (*Photo by Trey Holroyd*)

For the record, at age 47, I'm *still* on my way.

As for Putter Boy, he stayed on my parents' mantle until I married my magical wife Ashley. After I married, dad was very specific about the fact that I should take Putter Boy with me, as I embarked on my new life, wherever that road was gonna lead me, and so I did.

I could never tell my dad no.

Putter Boy sits on my mantle to this day, as I write these words, and that's right where he belongs. After all, he symbolizes all the time and effort and love my parents gave to me so I could chase my dream of being the best golfer in the world. I give him knucks every morning before I leave for work. My kids look at me like I'm crazy when I do it. Maybe that's because I am.

Hard to believe it's been over 30 years. I've aged, but Putter Boy looks the same.

If only I could get him to talk.

Chapter 8

BULLS BAY GOLF CLUB

Awendaw, South Carolina

7,014 yards

By Peter Cotton, the fellow who hopes he's done his best to heal sick folks, has seen his share of golf courses, and has loved every one of them

I love hilly golf courses, maybe because I grew up on one in Herefordshire, England. Oops, two untruths already in the first sentence.

The truth is, I am still struggling to grow up, and the golf course—Wormsley—was not nearby. It was 12 miles away, a long haul on my bicycle, up and down hills, carrying my few hickory clubs over my shoulder. Several lemonades were required.

Dad was a country doctor in general practice, not a golfer, but he eventually took a partner, Doug Chandler, who was keen and kind enough to take me out to Wormsley or Kington on Wednesdays, during school holidays, with the local vicar.

My Mum's father, whom I called "Gruncle" (I got confused between uncles and grandfathers at an early age), was a scratch golfer. He gave me some lessons and bequeathed me his first and favorite golf book *The Complete Golfer*, by Harry Vardon, published in 1909, and still gracing my coffee table. On the flyleaf Gruncle had penciled in some of his scores and his rapidly declining handicap. From that book I learned about cleeks and mashies and niblicks and rutting irons (for chipping out of the tracks of passing stage coaches), as well as the importance of wearing braces (a.k.a. suspenders) instead of a belt, and how to manage a stymie. At that time, and indeed into my teens, "bogey" was what we now call "par."

Not sure how and why that changed.

Six decades later I am living in the flat part of South Carolina known as the Low Country. There were no hills for miles until Mike Strantz designed a most wonderful golf course, Bulls Bay, some 15 years ago. Heaven knows how many millions of tons of earth were moved, but the clubhouse now sits on the highest point for hundreds of miles around. From the bar we can see 14 of the holes, and the view extends across the marsh to the ocean and to Dewees Island where I live. Someday I shall be content simply to sit on the Founder members patio and watch the youngsters struggling up the hill to the 18th green, like the "Oldest Member" in P. G. Wodehouse's wonderful tales of 1920s golf.

Bulls Bay is a true links course and stands comparison with my favorites around the world. There are so many great courses in the United States, and I have been humiliated on many of them. Too many to name them all, but in my dreams I replay outstanding rounds at Bandon Dunes (my idea of golf heaven), Cypress Point, Pasetiempo, Whistling Straights, Oakmont, and our nearby Kiawah Island Ocean course. Talking of humiliation, on my first round at Augusta National I took 27 putts (on the first 9 holes). On another occasion, Joe Bowden, Tripp's dad, and I played 63 holes there in one day.

I also have many favorite courses overseas. Not least Ballybunion, Tralee, Waterville, Doonbeg in Ireland; Turnberry and Carnoustie in Scotland; Cape Kidnappers, Kinloch, Jacks Point, and Kauri Cliffs in New Zealand; and Barnbougle Dunes, Lost Farm, and La Perouse in Australia.

. . . .

Bulls Bay is simply and proudly a golf club, not a fancy country club with tennis courts, swimming pools, coat and tie dining, or attentive knicker-wearing college kids patrolling the parking lot. We are fortunate to have a visionary owner, Joe Rice, who was able to recruit the best professional staff imaginable, including the legendary Terry Florence ("Flo") as the first manager and the iconic architect Mike Strantz. Sadly, both Flo and Mike have recently passed, but their influence and traditions persist. Rickey Sullivan is the marvelous director of instruction, who can even straighten out my game, if only temporarily. Lea Anne Brown manages the membership to a tee, and the course is always in great shape, thanks to Kenny Orlinger and his team.

My golfing memories at Bulls Bay and at other famous links are tempered and indeed enhanced by the fun I've had golfing in less familiar places. As a Professor of Medicine I have been privileged to travel widely to teach, at last count in over

Oh, the unexpected joys that go with victory in the Senior Men's Club Championship at Bulls Bay. There's nothing quite like a ride on our mascot, Titleist, the bull! (*Photo by Lea Anne Brown*)

50 countries, ranging from Argentina to Zimbabwe. Especially in the early days, my hosts squeezed the most out of me every day, so I insisted on playing golf, to get some time off. I also sometimes invented long lost relatives that had to be visited. That worked well in Australia, but was less convincing in Japan or China.

In India they were sneaky, and we teed off at 5 a.m., so as not to reduce my workday. I was not in perfect condition, having helped to celebrate the Queen's official birthday at the British Embassy. I can still feel, hear, and smell the Delhi dawn. Each of our foursome had 4 assistants—a caddy, a ball tee-er-upper, and a forward boy on each side of the fairway to (hopefully) find the ball, protect it from vultures and monkeys, and maybe adjust the lie.

I spent some time in Iran and the Gulf countries in the 1970s. The original engineers for the oil companies were all Scots, and each had laid out little 9-hole courses with browns instead of greens. The course I played had a man dozing beneath an umbrella next to each brown, waiting to roll it after each putt. One had a sign saying "Please replace the flag gently, otherwise you may strike oil and ruin the course."

My wife Marion and I played in Malaysia, where the highlight was someone carrying an umbrella to protect her from the harsh sun. That worked well until she started to give Marion advice, which her official caddy deeply resented. They were eventually separated. We also played in China a long, long time ago, when there was only one course in that whole huge country. Now there are fantastic resorts there attracting golfers from all over the world!

But mostly, when I think of time spent on the course, it's right back home in South Carolina, at Bulls Bay Golf Club.

In fact, I need a partner at Bulls Bay this afternoon. Care to join me?

Chapter 9

PALMETTO GOLF CLUB

Aiken, South Carolina

6,105 yards

By Tripp Bowden

Golfers in the know consider Palmetto Golf Club the second oldest club in America, just a few years behind Chicago Golf Club and the *very* hidden jewel Oakhurst Links (*both* are the oldest, depending on who you ask). I like to say Palmetto is *one* of the oldest, because to say second means you're not first, but to say you're *one* of the oldest means you're right there in the mix.

That ain't a bad place to be.

Built in 1892 as a three-hole golf course with three sets of tees per box (to make 9 holes played twice, which gives you 18), to experience the Palmetto is like going back in time, with no need for the capsule. Palmetto boasts, for the most part, dime-sized, crowned greens, and its clubhouse mirrors that of Shinnecock (small wonder, considering the same architectural firm—McKim, Mead and White—designed both). But none of this is what makes Palmetto so incredibly once in a lifetime special.

In fact, the answer just might surprise you.

Palmetto's reason for being was born out of necessity, though not because Southern folk had a hankering for putting a peg in the ground (or in this case a small mound of sand—the golf tee wasn't invented until 1889) and ripping a gutta-percha into the setting sun. Palmetto was built as a recreational playground for wealthy northerners with time on their hands and money in their pockets, northerners who spent their winters in the South because it was just too damn cold back home!

There were no planes back then and cars were hen's-teeth-rare (not that you'd want to travel across half a dozen states in one of those steam-spewing contraptions even if you had one), so the train was the way to go. The train that ran north and south, up and down growing America, whistle-stopped in none other than Aiken, South Carolina.

Aiken was the end of the line. Sunny Florida would have to wait, and that is how Palmetto Golf Club came to be.

Sort of.

• • • •

During the Depression, when most of America was trying to figure out where their next meal was coming from and if it was even worth eating, there was little fun to be found and seemingly no hope for a brighter tomorrow. Yet Robert Tyre Jones Jr., a.k.a. the legendary Bobby Jones, and a New York investment banker named Clifford Roberts who knew heavy hitters, decided to build their dream golf course a coincidental 30 minutes west of Palmetto.

All to bring back hope.

For their golf course architect, they chose to employ the unparalleled skills of Scotsman Alister MacKenzie, fresh from designing Cypress Point, what many consider perhaps the finest of all American golf course designs, or even one of the finest in the world. MacKenzie, known for leaving his mark with unforgettable signature *design* holes (see the slim-to-none-chance-for-birdie #5 at Augusta National), signature *natural* holes—as if God designed the hole and not MacKenzie (see the majestic #13), and signature *greens* (see the un-puttable #14), would soon work the same sort of magic at Palmetto.

As many members of Palmetto became members of Augusta, appreciating the keen design eye of MacKenzie and the many hands and heavy equipment that made it happen, they politely asked Mr. Roberts and Mr. Jones if perhaps, just perhaps, this MacKenzie fellow could come across the Savannah River to Aiken, South Carolina, and finish this great idea that began in 1892. And just like that (well not *exactly* like that; unforgettable greatness takes time), the Palmetto we know and love today was reborn and eventually raised, complete with signature hole #3, 4-puttable hole #5 (yes, I have done that many times and I consider myself pretty damn handy with the Billy Baroo), and most naturally designed hole, the par 3 7th, considered one of the top 100 holes in American Golf by the powers that be. . . . Whoever the heck they are.

But that's not what makes Palmetto so unforgettable.

If I could only play one last round of golf before the Grim Reaper with scythe in hand and a wedge in the other takes me home, it would be here.

Part of the magic that is Palmetto takes place even before you arrive, while still in your car, after a belly full of breakfast at the Track Kitchen located less than a mile down the road, with good ol' Pockets and family manning the spatula. Might I recommend to you two eggs sunny side up, real-buttered toast that literally melts in your mouth, grits that redefine the word (or is that world?), three slabs of salt-cured bacon, and all the proper coffee you can drink?

Please tell Pockets Tripp sent ya! And tip Pockets well.

It's passing by beautiful night-black race horses, so athletic in their gait it takes your breath, and you wish you could run like them, if only just once.

It's cruising beneath a canopy of loblolly pines and towering oaks into a pine straw parking lot, styling in your hand-me-down-from-your-mama's wickedly cool '79 Pontiac Grand Prix, black with silver pinstripes, with whitewall tires and chrome spoke rims, like something out of the 1920s.

It's John and Pat, Dennis and Kevin, cart boys even though they are grown men, men who double as locker room attendants and shoe shine magicians, but neither of those words do those fellows justice. That's like saying Shakespeare was just a gent who could write a little, someone who could put quill to paper and jot down a word or two.

It's John always greeting you with a hug and a "Man, it's so good to see you, Tripp—I been missing you. How you been?" At Palmetto, a hug is a hug, like the kind you get from Grandma.

You smile and John smiles, and you pop the trunk on that old school '79 Pontiac Grand Prix. John grabs your sticks and straps them to the back of a no-topper golf cart. He knows that's the kind you love, getting the wind in your hair and southern sun on your skin as you accept the challenge of one of the best golf course designs on the planet.

Before you tee off, John snags your golf shoes and shines 'em up bright enough to blind, like you're ready for the PGA Tour, even though he knows it'll be a great day for you if you go low, and by low I mean 75, not 65. (But John knows too, like you, that the numbers written on that score card don't matter. Not in the least.)

John shines those babies up before and aft, your street shoes, too, even if they are sneakers, Nikes or Adidas, because he wants you to look your best coming and going. And thanks to John, you do.

Also thanks to John, your cart coolers (yes, there are *two* of them) hang on the sides, both right and left like pocketbooks and purses on a rich girl's shoulder. They are full of beer and soft drinks and whatever else John thinks you might want, or need. Ginger ales for you are a given, because that's what Ben Hogan drank to make his hands feel thin when he gripped the club, and as a kid you wanted to be Hogan, and John knows all this. There are salted Planters Peanuts (Planters, because they remind you of your grandfather, Papa, who you miss something fierce, especially how he used to eat those peanuts or "goobers" as Papa liked to call them—John knows this, too). Nabisco malt crackers fill the cup holders, and there is a cold wet towel to start off with, draped on your bag, to wipe down your clubs (and soon the tears from your eyes) after your first chunked shot.

There is *always* a first chunked shot.

Palmetto is all this, and so much more. Palmetto is not just a course founded by members who stopped where the train told them to and later became members of hallowed Augusta National. No. Not even close.

It's warming up on the practice tee with half-flight golf balls, because the driving range at Palmetto is not really a driving range per se, but a small open space between

Me and Papa on the 18th green. What I wouldn't give to be with him there right now. (*Photo courtesy of Joe Bowden*)

the cart barn and the 17th and 18th fairways. When you boom your best drive it goes not 270 but 170, feathering the loblolly pine tree needles canvassing the end of said range, but not the tree itself. Not sure if even the mighty Dustin Johnson could clear those towing pines with half-flight balls. If I were a betting man, I would say no.

And I bet I would win.

It's changing into your golf shoes in the original clubhouse locker room, the one the gents from Shinnecock designed, the one in which your dad has a space. His locker is to the right as you walk in, granted kindly by the old "professor" and caretaker of Palmetto, Tommy Moore, a true ambassador of the game. Tom's lovely wife Cathy (she gives grandma-worthy hugs and has a smile for the ages), will hook you up with hot dogs and chips, Goo Goo Clusters, and whatnot. Her chili challenges Ms. Douglas's, from the Cabbage Patch, and that speaks volumes.

• • • •

Griever, me, the ol' Professor, and Pop, enjoying a moment of reflection on the knoll back of the 18th green. Special times. (*Photo by John*)

It's the first 5 holes at Palmetto, with nary a par 5 or par 3 in the mix, just a slew of beastly 4s, a stretch considered by the legendary Ben Hogan to be the 5 hardest starting holes in *all* of golf. I concur with Ben 100%. When and after you play your way through them, I bet a dollar to a doughnut you will agree, too.

Speaking of doughnuts, there is no such thing as a halfway house at Palmetto, no little building at the turn with sliding glass windows and a disinterested lady taking your order. There was no such thing back in 1892, and there is no such thing now, never will be. Palmetto keeps with tradition, and that is a very good thing.

Speaking of tradition and good things, make that *great* things, let's go back to John.

After you putt-out on 9, and before you can stripe your drive into the middle of the 10th fairway, or snap it into the unforgiving loblollies covered in Spanish Moss and chiggers, John is there with still-warm chili dogs (he wraps them in tin foil), restacked cart coolers, and anything else you could ask for. John is everywhere, yet coming out of nowhere.

It's the memory of winning the Devereaux Milburn with your dad in '98, the year you married your childhood sweetheart. Your dad, the good Doctor, stakes his round-changing 82-yard Ping gap wedge to 4 very makeable inches on the downhill, par 5 Crazy Creek 14th, for a 5 net *4* on second day Sunday, to all but seal the victory deal.

A shot for the ages.

It's the smile on the old professor's face when he hands you an envelope full of cold hard cash, winnings from the HAT POOL, because your dad bought your team, a team no one else would touch, thinking y'all had no chance in Hell because you, the ex-college golfer turned New York copy writer hadn't been playing much, hadn't been practicing. Well, they forgot about Doc. But *I* didn't.

It's winning the Islen Cup, ten years later, and good ol' John taking your picture with Doc's Nikon camera (this was *long* before cell phones had such remarkable capabilities); you and your dad, arms on shoulders standing peacock proud on the back crest of the par 3 16th green. The sun is setting behind you and y'all are sipping cold beer from the trophy cup you're holding, hand in hand, the sunlight bouncing off the silver, like when the plastic water glass on the dashboard vibrated in the original *Jurassic Park*.

That cup, that silver cup that means so much to you right now, will one day hold random coins and pocket lint and your baby girl's hair bands and who knows what else as your kids grow up and out of the nest.

But for now that silver plated trophy cup holds the memory of a lifetime, and that suits just fine.

It's sitting on the rocking chair front porch overlooking the 18th green, overlooking one-hundred-plus year old Cypress trees fading into the sunset that don't grow all that tall but *out,* like a big, beautiful, evergreen umbrella. It's walking over to those Cypress trees and asking them in all seriousness (yes, I have done that before): *What am I going to be when I grow up?*

And their answer is: *We don't know, kid. That's up to you.*
But we do know this: You're gonna be just fine.

Chapter 10

THE LINKS AT OVERTON PARK

Memphis, Tennessee

2,222 yards

By Turner Simkins, author of the life-changing book *Possibilities*, the story of how my son Brennan miraculously beat stage 4 Leukemia—our family gives so many thanks for all the prayers that friends, loved ones, and even strangers sent our way. We could *never* thank y'all enough.

To say we were in a drought is a three-dimensional understatement. No one in western Tennessee and Mississippi had seen rain in what seemed like months.

It had been a long, cold, and dry winter, both in our lives and in our weather, and here it was mid-March, and even the newly hatched daffodils, which have always served as my first whisper of the affirmation of Spring, had hung their heads with an unusual lack of spirit and color.

Back home in Augusta, I grew up leaning on the proverbial dogwoods/azalea combo as my barometer for how bright the new season would be. But finding ourselves stuck in Memphis while my middle son Brennan was in the midst of his fourth fight for his life at St. Jude Children's Research Hospital, I was interpreting these ashen blossoms as evidence of a pending dry and rainless stretch, thereby presaging all sorts of negative thoughts.

I was a mess.

My middle son Brennan was diagnosed with AML—typically an adult form of leukemia with a grim survival rate for kids—on his 7th birthday, 18 months earlier. As a young buck, Brennan served as the light of everyone's lives, including his older and younger brothers, always taking the first leap into a number of directions, which

Brennan at his absolute, beautiful best—showcasing his deep and endless love of the game—of golf *and* life. (*Photo by N. Turner Simkins*)

included many sports, but particularly golf, to which his two siblings and best friends quickly followed suit. I have a photo of Brennan swinging a small plastic golf club one Christmas morning (outside, in his pajamas, wearing a Tibetan skull cap, head down, hands out front, with his hips directing the yellow golf ball straight as straight can be) that anyone who knows anything about golf has looked at and said, "How in the world did he learn that move at that age?"

Brennan was more than a prodigy in that his sweet demeanor, combined with a merciless competitive spirit, transformed this beautiful little boy into a local bell cow for the game, encouraging not only his brothers, but scores of other friends and kids from his school to want to be like him. With his older brother Nat and baby brother Christopher (all three just 36 months apart) soon following suit, I found myself, like any proud dad dreaming about Green Jackets and Claret Jugs shared between a band of brothers. But when it came to Brennan, it was more of a belief than a dream.

So, on that cold January afternoon when we walked onto the fifth floor of the Georgia Children's Hospital, greeted by a baldheaded ten-year-old holding an overburdened IV pole, I was embarrassed to admit that the first thing to enter my mind was, "What if Brennan is never given the chance to show the world his amazing golf game?"

How's that for a thought when your kid is rendered a potential death sentence?

• • • •

On this afternoon, the dry cold seemed to change to a sticky warm. Being but a stone's throw from the mighty Mississippi, you don't need rain to create humidity. Brennan was in the bone marrow transplant unit (BMT Unit) at St. Jude for about three weeks after his fourth allogeneic bone marrow transplant (meaning fourth transplant with four donors), frail, pale, and literally hanging on until we were given a sign either that the transplant worked and he was going to achieve another remission, or that we would be planning for the worst. To say that this state of limbo created an overwhelming pall over our world is to just paint a picture of my mood, at that time, with a single black crayon.

Keeping up Brennan's competitive spirit was the best weapon he had at that time in this ghastly match against cancer. In addition to the fact that we could not allow

Brennan to see that we were literally worried sick, we also had to put on our best game faces for his brothers. But, by this time, our boys had said goodbye to more than a handful of kids in our cancer community to whom they had become very close. While we never talked about it, they knew what was at stake and were doing everything they could, even at that young age, to keep their chins up and stay positive.

Not an easy thing to do.

Just a few days before this latest transplant, Nat (10) and Christopher (7) were exposed to a virus at the little Montessori school into which we parachuted that previous fall—meaning none of us could visit Brennan in the BMT. So after school every day, we found ourselves seeking whatever form of distraction we could to keep our minds preoccupied and hearts filled with hope and each other.

Despite the uncomfortableness of the day, it was finally warm enough to do something outside.

Christopher's outdoor education teacher at his school was an amazing guy named Fletcher Golden. Though pushing 60, Fletcher is still an all-around great athlete, a man of many talents and skills, and a guy who had lost his older brother and best friend to leukemia years ago, when he was Christopher's age. While we had already learned a lot of cool stuff about Fletcher, it was about this time of year that he started discussing a different topic than usual—the Masters.

On this particular afternoon, Fletcher was standing in his usual spot outside the school pickup area when I arrived to gather my sons.

As I parked the car and walked up to see Fletcher, I noticed that he was rendering a pretty solid and fluid practice swing with none other than an ancient 1-iron. He looked up to address me. "Hey, Turner—you ever hit one of these things?" This, of course, was answered with my reference to Lee Trevino's Johnny Carson Show crack about lightning, God, and the 1-iron. By this time, my sons noticed what Fletcher was holding, and quickly the conversation turned to golf and how stupid we were to find ourselves at the beginning of spring without our golf clubs. But Fletcher quickly alleviated my regret with a statement that he had the rest of these clubs, plus a couple of spares in the back of his truck.

"So why don't we head out to Overton Park and give it a go, fellas?"

The boys and I were immediately on the back of that bandwagon.

Local muni The Links at Overton Park was literally just a couple of blocks from Target House, which is the long-term patient housing for families like ours entrenched at St. Jude for an indefinite amount of time. Overton is "the Old Forest," literally the place of the title to Peter Taylor's (one of the finest 20th century writers) beautiful book of stories about Memphis and the fading gentility of the old South. I'm just guessing, but I think Overton is well over 500 acres, as well as home to the Memphis Zoo, multiple ball fields, Frisbee parks, lakes, and an ancient, 9-hole golf course (built in 1912), which naturally meanders through the beautiful grassland and the old forest as if it had been there from the beginning.

As one who is drawn to old growth forests, particularly old growth hardwood settings where golf courses are involved, this is perhaps one of the most beautiful ancient stands of timber in the South. And it sits right smack dab in the middle of the town of Memphis.

• • • •

We arrived at Overton Park around four in the afternoon and parked outside the abandoned, Tudor clubhouse, which I had always wanted to pick up and move to my favorite public course back home. Leaning into the back of Fletcher's truck as we sifted through his assortment of old blades, including a couple of 1980s-era knock-off Pings, I called my wife, Tara, who was with Brennan in the BMT unit, to see how Brennan felt and if there was any news.

"Still no signs of engraftment," she stated with some concern, "but I'm looking out the window over the river and see some clouds on the horizon. I can't believe it, but it looks like it's finally going to rain. And with that, I have to be hopeful that something good is brewing inside his little body."

With my firm attention still on Tara's meteorological observation, I heard Fletcher tell the boys that we would each take two clubs and two balls. So with my cell phone wedged between my shoulder and right ear, I found a sand-wedge and a seven-iron, figuring that I could putt with the wedge (a practice I like to do on occasion to make sure I keep my head still with my putter). Glancing up through light green leafy buds on the oaks and maples towering overhead, I saw what Tara was referring to.

"You're right," I said. "And I feel it. The boys and I are with Fletcher, who brought us to Overton Park for a little golf outing. Sounded like a good idea and a great thing to do to keep the boys positive. Of course, it will only be our luck that the first day we decide to play golf we get rained and lightninged out."

"Well, I certainly don't want you being foolish with the boys and lightning," she replied, "but I think having your game messed up by the rain wouldn't be a bad thing. Still, ya'll have fun and enjoy the day, and make sure you call Brennan and tell him how it went!"

My wife Tara is not a golfer, but she loves the game and knows more about it, the rules, and the major players, than many friends of mine who actually do play. Just last summer, when Brennan achieved his first remission after transplant number one, we got him back out into the local Junior Tour the very moment we got the green light from the docs. And between transplants three and four, Brennan was actually begging to go to the golf course, despite the fact that his legs had grown so skinny he could hardly hold up his own weight.

Having learned about this special kid who madly loved golf, the nice folks at Memphis Country Club let me bring him by, where I maintain some of my proudest memories of this frail, little bald person, wearing a bright blue HEPA mask to keep out pollutants and allergens, stepping up to the matt and hitting his first iron shot in months, right down the pipe. It was a miracle he could even stand upright, much less hit it like an in-shape champ.

• • • •

While the dark clouds overhead began to shield the heat of the sun, it was still strangely humid as we embarked upon the shaggy bluegrass fairways with an unorthodox game plan. Not really knowing how we would structure a bet, and knowing my boys didn't have the ability to make good on one, we all decided that we would play a best ball for Brennan, and hopefully report back to him with an aggregate score that made him smile and even more determined to "beat cancer" and get back out on the links.

My first swing underscored the pervasive stickiness outside like a fat, tired bear emerging from hibernation. The short 200-yard par 4 was flat and wide, so a fat cut did not really hurt me too much as far as having a reachable second shot in, but a skulled punch and an up-up and down-down gave me a more than rough start. The boys did not fare much better. Christopher's expectation to come roaring out of the gate resulted in complaints that it was impossible to play golf with only two clubs.

Nat remained his calm, big brother self, but Christopher's near-tears rebuttal to every reassurance we could provide began to chink away at his withering psyche.

Walking off the green, which had not been cut that season, primarily due to the fact that the ancient Bermuda grass had yet to grow and was still mostly brown, it looked like the round was about to turn into more of a babysitting event than a nice day on the links. Fortunately, Fletcher quietly walked off the green, put a comforting hand on Christopher's shoulder, and said, "You know, I had a par. The team is ok."

"Team" is a term Christopher had yet to grasp at that young age. Always being the one left out, and often overlooked, particularly since his brother with cancer was always the focus, and his older brother was actively participating in church league basketball that winter, I recognized that Christopher wanted to shine for his buddy, Mr. Fletcher.

He was overdue for praise, but his first hole looked as if he was more talk than game.

On the following par 3, I actually managed to get up and down for par. Christopher continued to lash out at Nat, who was trying to help him with his swing. I felt that Fletcher was feeling as if he was butting in on a "family matter." Wanting to find an opportunity to regroup, I asked the two boys to have a seat along the cool wooded path that led to the 3rd hole. Fletcher walked on.

I heard thunder in the far distance.

My two boys sat down on a massive tree trunk, which showed rings that established witness to what had been a rural outpost to the city of Memphis in the late 1800s.

"You know, guys, Mr. Fletcher has gone out of his way to give y'all a special day, and you know how much he wants you to enjoy your first round of golf in a long time." I was speaking to them both, but this was mostly for Christopher. "And it looks like it may start lightning which will cut this day short, so let's forget about our individual scores and remember that we're all in this together. Just like we are all here in Memphis for Brennan, let's try to support each other. Listen to each other. Enjoy this beautiful place and know that each of us can play golf well and that it may take a hole or two to get a feel for it."

Christopher cried the most beautiful tears, hugged me, and held my hand as we walked through the towering forest to a beautiful lush opening. The sides of the fairway were accentuated by long wispy patches of broomsedge and native grasses, reminding me of a Monet painting or a bucolic pasture outside some magnificent British estate home. I told the boys we could all use each other's clubs, so each used the lone three-wood in our eclectic collection and proceeded to hit fine, straight tee shots, almost to the green of the next short par 4. I found myself back in the woods to the left, looking for my ball. With my search ending in vain, I declared my ball to be "in the linen" and met the boys on the next tee.

Both boys were beaming—Nat with a birdie and Christopher with a par (albeit with generous gimmies per Mr. Fletcher).

The next three holes winded back and forth through this pasture area, bordered with massive chestnut oaks around the greens and tees. As a group, we were 1-under par. Not bad—not bad at all.

The seventh at Overton was an uphill, long par 4 (300 yards, long for Overton Park). Nat's shot went wide right. But taking a 9-iron over the tree to the right of the green, I saw his ball land on the front fringe and take two bounces into the cup.

"EAGLE!! Daddy, I just made my first eagle ever!" Nat exclaimed, triggering jealousy with Christopher, but opening his eyes to the fact that this may be a special day indeed.

"I think we may actually turn something in to make Brennan proud," said Nat, beaming. "OK, Christopher. Now it's your turn."

On the eighth, the boys and I all made pars. Fletcher birdied. The air became suddenly cool, and I felt the ozone deliver a smell that I interpreted as a threat of lightning and rain. The sky was now dark, but I saw no single ominous cloud.

"We can finish boys! I don't want to rush and mess it up, but only one of us needs to par to turn in a 4 under for our soldier back at St. Jude!"

Nat, being only 10, lined up and ripped the shared 3-wood 230 yards, down the hill, over the creek (which I initially assumed to be daunting) but also over the green, his ball coming to rest under a hard, packed mulch area from another one of the large chestnut oaks. Christopher nailed his shot clothesline-straight, clearly over the creek, but 100 or so yards short of the green. Fletcher and I were also out there, but right and left respectively.

My two boys fist-bumped and proudly marched down the hill, clearly unaffected by my concern of distant lightning on the horizon and what was quickly looking like the arrival of a long overdue squall. Fletcher caught up to the two boys to congratulate them and express his impression of their skills.

I held back for a minute to collect my thoughts.

Looking off the tee box back towards town, I knew that this respite was about to be over and I was overcome with a feeling of foreboding. With the change in the weather and my concern for Brennan constantly bubbling under the surface, it felt as if we were on the cusp of weighty news. By the time I reached the car, I just knew we would have a voice mail or text from Tara with material information as to whether these two fine young golfers would have a brother with a chance to live before they arrived back at Target House.

The impending storm represented to me the physical manifestation of a climate that would deliver either relief for this old forest, or possible destruction. The ambiguity of life's cycles demonstrates power that can both feed and destroy.

As I plodded down the hill and onto the fairway, I found myself fixated on the grass beneath my feet. Each blade of grass represented both beauty and substance to this uniquely picturesque and quietly historic golf environment, like the individual cells of an ecosystem that was teetering on the balance of either burnout or restoration. It had been literally months since this place had been fed with water and it was at its own critical juncture. The earth under our feet was gasping for solace, as my son Brennan's new little immune system was desperate to either take new root or disappear forever.

Keeping my thoughts to myself, I watched as Christopher delivered his wedge shot safely on the green, but I found Nat somewhat troubled by a tricky pitch shot under the low hanging limbs of a massive oak, uncertain he could produce the necessary concentration to run his shot up on the green and keep it there. But when I saw his quiet determination steady his head and hands behind the ball, I felt as if everything overshadowing our day and our lives was to be determined by his ability to pull off this shot.

Rhythmically delivering a mid-iron to the center of the golf ball, Nat nailed the perfect low running pitch up and through a minefield of acorns and roots, into the fringe, onto the green and, with one last rotation of the ball, into the hole for birdie and a total of 5-under par for Brennan!

I do not know if I imagined it or if it really happened, but I can almost swear that as the ball fell into the cup, we felt the sharp, short boom of a thunderclap. Rain began to fall, not in a devastating downpour, but in a gentle, steady shower. In that instant, we witnessed the deliverance of nourishment and comfort to this small corner of the golf world. And with it, I was offered hope for this band of brothers who had never lost their passion for a game that means so much more to them than just a few hours together after school.

• • • •

A grueling four months later, Brennan himself arrived at this sacred place—The Links at Overton Park, a place where children from the inner city are provided the opportunity to learn a game that would otherwise be inaccessible, and a place where the true lover of the game of golf can realize that there is so much more to a meaningful game than a fancy club and an immaculate facility. To me, it is rare to find what many would call a "goat track" that is this stunningly beautiful. Overton is a place to feel the game at its raw essence. The forest itself is more than a sufficient playing partner.

This particular afternoon, unlike the last time we were here at Overton, was pure blue skies and sunshine. The azaleas and dogwoods were now trumpeting the birth of a new season, and discussions of drought had been relegated to old newspaper bins.

We pushed Brennan around those nine holes in a wheelchair, but only as a means of transportation, and to save what little energy he had. Brennan eagerly and happily allowed his brothers to recap every shot of their five-under par round dedicated to him on that unsettling afternoon. And, with his ubiquitous HEPA filter face-mask and shiny, bald head, that unflappable little soldier managed to hit every shot and finesse every putt necessary to let the world know that a competitive spirit never dies.

His remission was strong and, while I may have pushed the boundaries established by his doctors in allowing him on the course at that time, I knew Brennan needed to be out there to tell his brothers he was back, and better than ever.

With our foursome now back together, we felt peace over the fact that no matter where we may be, as long as we are together in spirit, we can truly experience the magnificence of life's greatest games.

God is good.

Chapter 11

TUPELO COUNTRY CLUB

Belden, Mississippi

6,887 yards

By Tripp Bowden

Tupelo, Mississippi, is famous for being the birthplace of two things. The first is well known, the second, not so much.

There's the birthplace of Elvis, and then there is the birthplace of my golf game, even though I had been playing for almost four years when I arrived at that magical place, fresh off a groggy, head-bobbing Greyhound bus ride from Little Rock, Arkansas, that took its own sweet time to get here.

Tupelo, Mississippi—quite the place to be born again.

This was in the days of the Sony Walkman, a unique device that allowed you to take your music with you wherever you were going, for the first time *ever*. Just pop in your favorite cassette (the CD wasn't even thought of back then), strap on George Jetson-looking head phones, and press play. Hit the Dolby button to drown out the hiss, and whether by design or not, that little Dolby button added a bit of extra bass and a touch of mid-range to keep the back-beat deep.

I like the back-beat deep, and apparently, I like it *really* loud.

I was rocking one of these Walkman devices, cranked up to ten (or was it eleven?), when the driver of our Greyhound pulled over to the shoulder of Highway 98 and squealed to a stop, interrupting my musical trance as I stared out a dirty window listening to Prince wail on his guitar and wax on philosophically about crying doves.

Feeling the bus jam to a halt I thought, *Oh damn! Flat tire?* I didn't hear it pop, though how could I with the music on my Walkman blasting and thumping so loud you'd think I was on my own personal tour bus, like Axl Rose (front man for all-time classic eighties rock band Guns N' Roses, who was so hated by his bandmates that they made him take his own bus!).

Except I'm *not* Axl Rose.

I was sharing this Grey Dog to Elvis's hometown with 60 other people, travelers just like me, though I was by far the youngest of the bunch, and when the driver came storming to the back (for those taking notes, he's a *lot* bigger than he looked sitting in the driver's seat as he welcomed me on board with a Barney Fife smile and a wave), I wondered why he's coming right at me. Like I was a beacon in the night, but not one offering hope.

Me? What did *I* do?

He's on me like a 300-pound spider monkey, snatching the Walkman off my ears, headphones flying. The music was really blasting now, and now I got it. With the eyes of all passengers now on me, our driver screamed at me in a voice that didn't match his gargantuan frame (his voice was strangely high-pitched, like a dog whistle, except you could hear it—oh man could you hear it!).

"Son, I have been trying to get your attention for the past twenty exits! You're not the only passenger on my bus today, gah'dammit! You need to turn that shit down! *Now!*"

"I'm so sorry, sir," I said, though I doubted that he could hear me. Not with the music playing so loud.

So I went one better. I didn't turn that shit down, I turned that shit *off*.

When our Grey Dog pulled back onto the highway and a silent two hours later into Tupelo's bus hub, I thought: what an auspicious start to what will go on to be the greatest 14 days of my young golfing life. Of course, I had no way of knowing that at the time, though that is exactly what happened.

For the next two weeks I would lay my head at the home of Mike and Rhonda Shannon, and their two young kids Tracy and Frank, who came and went like ping pong balls without the paddle. Great kids, though I rarely saw them, busy as they were with the bountiful joys of being a kid.

You might remember Mike from earlier in the book. He was the assistant professional at Augusta National, who gave me my first ever golf lesson on the east practice tee, the Monday after the '77 Masters, when Tom Watson won for the very first time. Mike was now a head golf professional for the very first time, fresh from his stint at Augusta National.

Tupelo Country Club was Mike's show, he's the man behind the curtain, and he had invited me out for the summer to play the game of golf and learn at the knee of the man who many considered one of the best teachers in the game, though Mike of course would never admit that he was. Trust me, he was.

• • • •

Since Mike was the head pro, mornings started damn early in the Shannon household. Call it Marine morning early, yet Mike's wife Rhonda was there in the kitchen at the ready, whipping up a kick-ass, southern-style breakfast of dreams. There were eggs over light, buttered toast, blackberry jelly if you wanted it, the real kind with the seeds still in it, and thick-cut peppered bacon (all you could eat), with a big glass of OJ to wash it all down).

And by glass, I mean Rhonda offerd you the whole jug. What a great way to jump-start the day for someone who is not even remotely a morning person. My dad often jokes that, "Tripp's heart doesn't start beating until noon!"

After breakfast and an unexpected but much appreciated sweet, have-a-great-day kiss on the cheek from Rhonda—a.k.a. the Big R (she is tall and stunningly beautiful in the fashion of Sophia Lauren, a pure Southern Belle and just genuinely sweet as can be), Mike and I tooled down mostly deserted unlit backroads in his poison-berry red, road-hugging Pontiac Firebird, with Mike raising his index finger at any and every passing car in a warm and welcoming morning wave. I didn't find this gesture odd but instead damn cool, even though outside it was dark as a bruised banana and the passing cars couldn't even see Mike's gesture.

How cool was this! Cruising down the Mississippi backroads of Elvis Presley's birthplace at the tender age of 16 with a man who would one day become the #1 short game golf instructor in the world. (Crazy, I know.) Sliding down moonlit backroads in a wickedly cool Pontiac Firebird with black leather bucket seats that comfort, because even though you're not wearing seatbelts and those seats were slicker than a used car salesman, those buckets held you in place. No such thing as seat belts back in the seventies—using them, I mean.

Man, this was cool beyond description.

When Mike gunned it to give the ol' girl some breathing room from stop sign to stop light, I could feel the engine in my bones, all the way to the marrow, the bone removed.

I blinked away my morning fog as we took the next of what seemed like many turns, and next thing I knew we emerged from a blur of grass, trees, and blacktop into the parking lot of Tupelo Country Club. There wasn't anybody here but us, or was there? There's a light on in the pro shop, a small glow that barely makes a difference.

A light on this early, when there was no light in the sky?

Quickly inside (Mike's a fast mover, a hit-it and get-it kind of guy, no dawdling around Mike's Oz), I was immediately greeted with a big ol' firm handshake by an assistant pro who went by the name of Diamond Jim, an older, gangly gent with hands like a boxer, standing tall and proud, who I later learned was a combat veteran with two wars under his belt, 4 former wives (hence the name Diamond), and had *never* swung a golf club in his life. Yowza!

You couldn't make this stuff up.

After this massive handshake before sunrise, Diamond looked at me and smiled a beautiful shit-eating grin, if a shit-eating grin could ever be beautiful (his was). And after more brief introductions Diamond looked down at me and said, "You must be somebody pretty damn special for Mike to bring you here all the way from Georgia. But just remember this, son. There ain't *no* rest for the weary, and the wicked don't *need* any."

I grinned like a goofy goober, looking around for Mike. I needed help. I wondered if I was wicked or weary. Guess I'd find out soon enough.

Soon enough came immediately.

As soon as I exited the golf shop and put my bag down on the rail outside, Mike yelled: "Don't put your bag down there, Pahds. Golf bag sitting on the rail won't do you any good."

Mike was standing on what he liked to call the frog hair, the fringe of the vast Tupelo Country Club putting green, which also serves as the chipping green, meaning you could work on your chips, your bump and runs, your pitches. It's also still dark as self-inflicted guilt outside, so I was not entirely sure what Mike was asking me to do.

If the sun wanted to rise, it wasn't showing any interest.

Diamond banged on the pro shop window, pointed at me, and flipped on the flood lights. If a bang on a window could ever say: Get your ass over *there!* (with *there* being where Mike is standing), this would have been it.

Mike smiled and began my new life with a simple, but exponential, lesson for the ages.

"Pahds, I want to teach you the best golf lesson ever taught to me. Taught to me by a fellow out in Texas, a gentleman by the name of Harvey Penick. He taught the game to Tom Kite and Ben Crenshaw—you may have heard of them. You also may have heard of the old adage: Practice make perfect. Your dad says you're pretty clever, so I reckon you have. Well, Pahds, that adage is a myth, an old wives' tale, and it is complete and utter bullshit. Practice does *not* make perfect. *Perfect* practice make perfect. Big, big difference."

I chewed on this and thought maybe I liked the taste, though at the time I was too young and stupid to have any idea what it truly meant.

Mike threw me a sleeve of Titleist 384s. "Don't ever play another ball," he said, with nothing more to add. This was affirmation. "Now grab that 8813 blade and come over here and let's roll a few."

I pulled my Wilson 8813 out of my Ping golf bag, the blade a mighty kind gift from a *Golf Digest* teaching pro out of Long Island, a fellow by the name of Mike Hebron, who had the entire back wall of his office lined with classic clubs, and this 8813 putter was one of them. I took a shine to it, my mom worked her southern magic, and next thing I knew that putter was mine: my girl for life.

Thirty-seven years later, that putter is still in my bag.

I walked over and looked down into the bulb-lighted darkness as Mike took a chalk line and stretched it out. One end at the hole, the other 3 feet away: the proverbial and dreaded 3-footer. Mike popped the string, and a three-foot white line magically appeared.

Mike looked me dead in the eye, like we were going to war.

"Master the three-footer. Master the three-footer and you can master anything. Hand me that sleeve of Titleists, please, sir."

Mike opened up the box, laid the golf balls side by side, three abreast, again looked me dead in the eye, smiled, and said: "50 in a row, Pahds. Make *fifty* in a row from three feet and we can move on to the next lesson. Miss *one*, you start over, even if it is number 49. Miss and you start over. Holler at me when you get there. Don't worry, you will. It may not be today, may not be tomorrow, may not even be the day after that, but I promise you you'll get there."

I looked up and away and saw that the sun had crept up into the sky like a wounded angel (or was that me?)—creeping up as if to say, "Man, I gotta see this!"

● ● ● ●

Perfect practice at Tupelo is quite the concept. Fifty three-footers in a row leads me to five five-footers in a row from 6 feet, then two in a row from 10 feet. Two putts in a row from ten or start over? Yowza, again! Then it's off to the edge of the green—30 feet out with a 7-iron—bump and run until you hole one out. Hole out your first attempt, and guess what? You are done with that drill for the day. But if one hundred attempts later you still haven't holed one out yet, your ass better keep going until you do. You could be there all day.

Tomorrow, too, for that matter.

Master the bump and run, said Mike, and by master, Mike meant hole-one-out, then it's off to the bunker—and always know it's a *bunker* not a sand trap, a hole and not a cup, a flagstick and not a pen. A pen is something with which you write, a cup is something from which you drink, and a sand trap is something you played in as a kid.

A two-time Walker Cup captain once taught me that, as well—though later in my golfing life—the bit about the bunker not being a trap, the hole not being a cup, the flagstick not being a pen. A gent named Jim Holtgrieve, 5-time Masters Tournament player, twice captain, and 3-time member of the Walker Cup team (back when such an honor garnered a coveted invitation to the Masters), as well as the inaugural Mid-Amateur champion. My goodness, could Jim hit a golf ball! Ripping a 1-iron with a club head the size of a Triscuit 275 yards, and this was back in the early eighties when golf clubs were still real and the ball didn't fly as if connected to a remote control. Sadly, the *flat* blade was not Jim's friend (he could shoot 66 without making a putt longer than his short left arm, but two-putting all the par 5s he hit in two), but 'Griever's ball-striking ability was like none I had ever seen, before, or since.

Mike again, his voice in my ear, brain, and heart, as I stepped back into the Tupelo Country Club practice bunker where he had left me half an hour ago, sunlight bouncing off the powdery sand like an eggshell mirror, reflecting onto my skin and into my eyes. *Pahds, in the bunker you settle in like you own it; dig those spikes in deep. Now choke down on the grip and open the blade up wide, angle it off your right shoulder, there you go, and only* then *do you set your grip. Lock your fingers in gently, then rip it hard as you can just a bump back of the ball and let the sand do the rest.*

I promise you, it will.

And then you pray like hell you hole one out, I said to myself, with the sun beating down on me like John Henry's sledgehammer.

After the bunker, it's the practice tee, where I had to hit two greens in a row out in the distance, and they were about the size of a dinner plate, from various and sundry *distances*, with every iron in my bag, sand wedge to the knife. But the woods, both driver and three, are all about parameters, not greens. Keep it between the navigational beacons five times in a row with those babies and your work here is done. The golf course awaited me, and I couldn't wait to get there.

And get there I did, in ways I didn't even know were possible.

Proof that perfect practice does make perfect, if only for that one magical summer in Tupelo, Mississippi. Thirty-five years removed from this swing sequence photograph, it is hard to believe this was really me. (*Photo by Mike Shannon*)

• • • •

My Tupelo Country Club great golf course experience could end here, but I can't close out this story without telling you about a match between a fellow teenager named Lan Gooch and myself, and the 10-footer on 18 for birdie that took him down. Gooch was a college golfer, a sophomore at vaunted Ole Miss, a Division I All-America player more than once, who would one day play on the PGA Tour, and was just a genuine good dude. He was also light years better than me.

Or so he thought.

After staring into my bag at a Ping Eye 2 4-iron, standing in the fairway of the 18th hole at Tupelo Country Club and looking out to the green 187 yards away, I was thinking, *You know, if I can hit one green* five *times in a row, and this, this is just* once. *If I strike it right, a makeable 10-foot birdie putt awaits, and if I can make two putts in a row from ten more times than not, then I got this. I got this.*

Yes sir, Mike Shannon. Your Tupelo Pahds has *got* this.

From the beauty of learning not how to just practice but learning *perfect* practice, and that only perfect practice makes perfect even in a very imperfect game, after my 4-iron from 187 yards out landed exactly that predicted ten feet away, I rolled my Titleist 6 into the hole like a rat sneaking out the kitchen door with no one looking. I knew that ball was going to disappear into that summertime Bermuda-grass green the moment it left the blade of my Wilson 8813. An experience I would never forget, and will recollect often when I am in the nursing home (should I make it that far).

Perfect practice makes perfect. You should try it sometime.

What I wouldn't give to try it again.

Chapter 12

POINTE SOUTH GOLF CLUB

Hephzibah, Georgia

5,508 yards

By Kate Mashburn, back-to-back state
championship winner, with dreams
of dental school and a job
with a dependable income

Though I have been playing golf for over 8 of the 17 years of my young life, I still consider myself a fledgling of the game. I know just enough to be dangerous, and just enough to know I know nothing at all.

I was introduced to the game at the spry age of 9, by my dad, Craig, who at the time of my introduction into the game could barely break 90 without an eraser and a sack of hammers. Dad is now scratch, painful as that is for his friends to believe—especially for the author, Mr. Tripp.

I should also mention my mom, Shawn, who made a hole-in-one the *very* first time she ever played a round of golf, and yet she never played golf again. One swing, one ace, and Mom was done. Just like the old comedy skit by Steve Martin, *One Show, Good-Bye*. Quite the golf lineage, you might say.

No wonder my golf life has been such a roller coaster ride.

• • • •

Junior lessons come frequently from the local pro at Fields Ferry Golf Club, a fellow named Eric Stewart who is nice as he can be and seems to really know his stuff, especially the way he can work his magic with me. Fields Ferry is a hilly and winding track just north of my hometown of Calhoun, Georgia, in an area known as The Carpet Capital of the World (might sound Dolly Parton country but it's true), and is just a fun place to grow up and learn how to play the game of golf.

• • • •

Most lessons from Eric are just the basics: grip, alignment, square this up, square that up, tight turn with your shoulders, Kate, now keep your head still. They're the basic lessons of golf that become the very foundation and fabric of my game for the rest of my life, though of course I don't know it at the time.

Keep your head still—I still don't know what that means. How is that even humanly possible, when you're swinging hard as you can while moving your body this way and that?

As I took a shine to the game of golf, Dad put me in US Kids tournaments, and I started really liking it, really enjoying the game and the simplicity of it all. Just hit a little white ball, see where it goes, go chase after it, and you get to ponder life along the way, which I thought was really cool, because I love to ponder life. So I dropped softball (the bigger white ball), dropped basketball (the even bigger brown one), and got really serious about the game of golf.

In fact, I dropped all the sports I loved, but undeniably not as much as I loved the game of golf.

It's funny, but I feel like I blinked and somehow became a pretty good golfer. I'm no Nancy Lopez or Annika Sorenstam (at least not yet), but I am good enough to win a state championship in high school as a sophomore, and now here I am with a chance to defend and win another. I am either very lucky, blessed, or both.

I'll go with both.

• • • •

The road to state.

The road to a state championship in golf or any other high school championship is an arduous one, no matter the level of play. At Calhoun High School we play Class 3A in all sports (the highest level in Georgia high school sports is Class 7A—Yowza!), and we are more often than not expected to win our share of trophies, so we were kind of expected to win region, which is step one to getting to the state championship. Most of the teams in our region (we're considered one of the best regions in the state of Georgia—who made that call, I don't know) make it to sectionals, which is the next rung on the ladder. If it sounds like a great accomplishment, don't be too impressed. All you have to do is break 300 as a team, as in with just your best three scores out of four. And in sectionals, it's about the same—a team score of 290, I think, and then it's off to the state championship you go, should your team find a way to shoot 290 between the four of you. But if you *win* region, which we did by a score I don't recall, you skip sectionals all together, and go straight to state—seems kind of ridiculous to me. I wouldn't call it a cake-walk to get to state, but there is a little too much Betty Crocker in it for my taste.

So with the region win in our back pocket, it's off to state we go.

State is a single-day event, which I love, because if I play well, play my heart out and the stars align, I just might get a chance to win it all individually.

Absolutely I'm a team player, but don't think for a second I don't want to beat every single player on that scoreboard.

But what makes state so special to me is not just getting there, but getting a chance to play Blessed Trinity, our dear archrivals who are equally as good as we are but have yet to beat us when it counts the most. I love playing against Hannah Jones, a great player who I started out the game with back in the US Kids' tournament days. Our scores are often similar enough to where we are in the same group together, and we get to have a lot of fun on the course, catch up ,and just be friends, in spite of what's at stake.

Hannah and I both know very well what is on the line.

We also know very well the condition of the golf course we are playing with the state championship on today's line. Terrible would not be fair to say, but the fairways at Pointe South are as baked out as a forgotten-in-the-oven Bundt cake and as hard as my 5th period Calculus class, with lies tighter than a skull cap!

• • • •

The boys' teams play really nice golf courses, compared to us girls, especially when it comes to events like region, sectionals, or state. For example, for region the boys play the aforementioned Fields Ferry Golf Club, a really nice layout, where I grew up learning the game (still learning, of course), while the girls play The Elks Club, which is a shade worse in condition than Pointe South, the course we are about to play today. And the boys get to play Fort Gordon for state, the Army base course, always in pristine condition. What a track that is, or so I am told . . . It's not like I will ever get a chance to experience it up close and personal, at least not in a state championship.

It doesn't seem fair—discriminatory, if you ask me. But that's another story for another time.

For this time, it's round one of state, the only round, actually, so it's all or nothing today, and with the sun rising into the sky as curious to the outcome as I am, my teammate Katie Kaufman tees off first, because she's our fourth player, and just rips one down the middle. Whoo-hoo!

Lead the way, Katie!

As my other teammates go off, group by respective group, with our number three player Maddie Crump followed by number two Katie-Rose Rawls, I can't help but get exponentially nervous, because I know what I'm capable of, and yes, sure, they could mess up, but I could mess up, too. Still, in spite of all this worry, I am very confident in myself. I've been in this situation before.

In spite of all my preparation leading up to this moment, I am still so nervous it's all I can do to put on my FootJoy golf glove, put a peg in the ground, and see what the day may bring. The sun probably knows more about it than I do.

Fast forward 6 hours.

Today is obviously not my best round of golf, seeing as I just shot 85. Small wonder the women's golf coach from Augusta State University stopped following me hours ago. A 45 on the front will do that.

I just shot an eighty-five. Wow.

I remember on the third hole, a short, seemingly pancake of a par 4, yet still I tried to play safe and not stupid. Why, I don't know. I hit a really good drive, just a wedge in, but my second shot went into the greenside bunker—I was even at the time, ready to go under. I consider myself pretty good at getting out of the bunker, greenside or otherwise, but somehow it took me 4 shots to get out. Four shots out of a greenside bunker! Take away any one of those blundered shots and we are not in a playoff to win the state championship. We would already be holding the trophy.

My front 9 continued on that way accordingly; I was in the tank pretty much start to finish, in spite of all my efforts to the contrary, though on the back 9 I managed to rally the troops and show some merit.

Sort of.

I was only 1-over on the back after a two-putt birdie on the par 5 16th, until I doubled the easy par 4 17th with a wedge in my hand.

Standing on the18th tee, a straight away par 3 playing about one-thirty and change, I know I have a chance to redeem myself after my double on the last, though of course I don't know by how much. Will a par seal the deal, or do I need a birdie? No one seems willing to tell me. Why won't they tell me?

I'm so mad at myself right now. Wish I had a nail to bite in half.

I take a deep breath and take my 7-iron and rip it with all that I have, dead on the flagstick, keeping my head still or not still. My tee shot lands just shy of the flag but bounces like crazy to the back of the green, hard as tarmac. I size up the putt to the best of my abilities, but the best of my abilities is embracing a grainy as it gets 40-footer, which turns into another equally grainy, but shorter, 10 footer for par that I miss, rolling it just past the edge. I tap in for bogey.

Dang. A bogey on the last.

I hate to bogey the last hole, regardless of circumstances or venues.

There are a lot of folks surrounding the green to cheer me on, and I am thinking although I hear no cheers, when I tap in for bogey I have no idea that *that* putt was for the win, not the tie. The *par* putt, not the *bogey* putt. My bogey putt was for the tie.

Kate: My preferred way to celebrate a most unlikely victory. Just me and the trophy, and mom with her trusty camera, capturing the moment. Not that I could ever forget a moment like this. (*Photo by Shawn Mashburn*)

Except I still don't even know that yet. All I know is that my round is over after 6 and a half grueling hours in the steaming South Georgia sun.

I see Hannah, my good friend who plays number one for Blessed Trinity, who I hear just shot 79 on this crazy track, and so I hug her neck and congratulate her. Breaking 80 on this pinball machine? Way to go, Hannah!

And then I go over to Coach Stephenson (the best coach a kid could ever dream of having) and ask, half-jokingly but with a full smile, "How'd we do, Coach?"

Coach gets real quiet, unusual for him, and then he says: "We're tied, Kate."

Oh, no. Affirmation. I prayed it wasn't true, even though I had a really bad feeling it was.

But let's back up. This may sound crazy, but around mid-season, during a match against North Murray High School, Coach had prepared us in the event of a potential tie.

We were having a lot of fun playing match play, a format we rarely get to play, though North Murray just wanted to play 9 holes and head back home. But Coach Stephenson said to their coach, "Well, since y'all drove all the way to Calhoun for a 9-hole exhibition match, why don't we play a little longer? Plenty of daylight left."

Their coach agreed.

As we readied for the back 9, Coach Stephenson said to us in all seriousness, "Alright y'all, pretend we just tied North Murray for the state championship. Do y'all know what to do, to get ready for a playoff? Of course our answer was no. Our group of players had never been in such a situation in our lives. So Coach Stephenson walked us through the format, and made us practice the rest of the way that day as if we would end up tied for state a few months down the road—a dress rehearsal, to know what to do, to be Marine-ready for a playoff, though I thought Coach's logic was kind of crazy at the time. No way was that ever gonna happen. A playoff for state?

Yet here we are.

Remember in the beginning when I told you I knew just enough about the game to be dangerous? Well, this is the time when I know just enough to know I know nothing at all. Although I *do* know how to ready myself for a playoff for the AAA state girls golf championship, thanks to the Nostradamus ways of Coach Stephenson.

With my family gathered 'round and a three-putt lump still stuck deep in my throat, I watch helplessly from the Pointe South sidelines as my teammates Katie and Maddie, paired with the number four and three players for Blessed Trinity, tee off and make their way down the fairway. I am, again, just as nervous as I can be, because there is absolutely *nothing* I can do to change the outcome of what is about to unfold ahead of me. Their group will play the entire first hole to the bottom of the cup, before Katie-Ross and I can so much as rip our drivers. That's the rule for a Georgia State Championship playoff, like it or not.

And then the roles will be reversed, with Katie and Maddie channeling our nervousness, knowing that there is absolutely nothing that *they* can do to change the outcome of what they are witnessing. It's as intense and helpless of a feeling you could ever have, at least for a 17-year-old kid.

I say that—though I'm sure there are such feelings out there that are equal and much worse for 17-year-old kids across America. In fact, I know there are.

• • • •

In my heart, I know I have to beat this girl (she's actually Hannah Jones, one of my best friends and my absolute favorite to compete against, regardless of the stakes), and when the whistle blows for us to tee off, we both rip one beautifully down the baked out Pointe South fairway. I cannot control what is in front of me, but I can control what is inside me.

Or can I?

The golf gods have a great sense of humor.

In spite of the pristine drives, we all make rather sloppy bogeys on the short par 4 first to push the playoff, but on the par 4 second, everything changes. It's the same format—y'all play while we wait, y'all wait while we play—but this time *everyone* in our group hits really good drives, and then the green, except for my teammate Katie-Ross. The three of us quickly mark our balls and step aside, trying to beat the approaching darkness. Katie steps in and chips it 10 feet short of the hole, not her best effort by any stretch, as Katie can flat out play, leaving herself an improbable downhill putt on a dried up, patchwork green that looks more like a moth-eaten quilt you'd find in your grandma's attic, than a green on a course hosting the 2016 AAA state championship.

All I could think was: Oh, my gosh—this is so bad, we're done. And when I roll my putt three feet past, tap in, I'm done, too. Par won't be enough; two-putts from the Blessed Trinity girls and the dream is over.

Hannah Jones, my good friend and fearless opponent, rolls her putt nicely but misses. Just barely, but a miss none the less, then taps in for par. I honestly thought Hannah was gonna make that one. She usually does.

Sarah, playing number two for Blessed Trinity, has a pretty short birdie putt, just outside of Katie's putt for par—think 12 feet instead of 10—but rolls it barely short of the hole, and for whatever reason she marks it. I'm a little surprised, but then think nothing more of it.

I am now thinking of all *my* worst case scenarios: what if this putt was made, what if that first bunker shot cleared the lip, what if, what if, but before I can conclude any of them Katie drains her un-makeable downhill, patch-quilt snake for par!

Now I'm thinking WOW! Next tee, next plans—we can still win this! Sarah's putt is a gimmie—a foot at the most. I reach for my bag, fully expecting Sarah to make it.

She doesn't. Sarah misses.

We just won the state championship.

I want to celebrate, but I can't. Neither can my teammates. This is not a time for celebration. This is a time for consolation—to comfort and console a dear friend and golfing comrade at one of the lowest points of her life (and one of the highest of mine—talk about a juxtaposition), golfing or otherwise. I know, I was just there, on hole number 18, not that long ago.

I walk over with tears in my eyes, and give Sarah a hug that won't let go.

None of us give a hoot and a holler. None of us celebrate. We just hug one another, teammates and opponents, family and friends. There aren't that many fans around—it's late and the course is closed, and it's time to go home.

Except it's not.

There will be trophies handed out, hugs around necks, stares into space and into the ground—even a ten-car police escort when we get back home to Calhoun to a toilet papered front yard. I cannot believe we just won a second state championship, back-to-dang-back, but I am most proud of the way we celebrated.

We didn't.

Chapter 13

SAND HILLS GOLF CLUB

Mullen, Nebraska

6,432 yards

By Adam Ikamas, CCGS, Executive Director of the Michigan Golf Course Superintendents Association, golf course superintendent by trade, husband to a magical woman by God's grace, and proud papa of two beautiful baby girls

One of the advantages, one of the unknowns about the superintendent side of the game is that just like a golf professional, be it a club head pro or a player on the PGA Tour, you can pretty much play golf wherever you want. Augusta National is not on that list, but just about any other place else is.

That's a pretty special perk if you love the game like I do.

Fortunately for me, the superintendent at the uber-exclusive but laid-back Sand Hills Golf Club—Kyle Hegland—is a good buddy of mine. We went to turf school together back in 2002, back when the world was young. Kyle is a Wisconsin Badger by birth but now an MSU Spartan to his bones. He and I shared notes at Michigan State and still somehow managed to find a way to graduate on time with turf degrees in our hot little hands. Fresh out of college, and as a frosh assistant superintendent, Kyle cut his turf teeth at Austin Golf Club for quite a few years, making a bit of a name for himself. Two-time Masters champion Ben Crenshaw is the touring pro at Austin Golf Club.

That's pretty cool. In fact, Ben and Bill Coore built the mythical Sand Hills Golf Club for sole owner Dick Youngscap back in 1995, and Kyle, being at the right place and the very right time, got the nod from Coore-Crenshaw to take over as head super. Ever since he got that job for the ages, Kyle has been saying to me: "You gotta get out here. You gotta get our here. Adam, you won't believe this place! And there's only *one* rule out here at Sand Hills. One rule!"

"And what might that be?" I ask.

"Don't be an asshole!"

Now *that* I can handle.

You gotta get out here, Adam. Not an easy task, seeing how Sand Hills redefines the phrase "the middle of nowhere."

• • • •

Unless you have a private plane, the fastest way of getting out to Sand Hills is to fly into Denver, Colorado, hop in a rental car, and drive five and a half hours northeast. The census for Mullen, Nebraska, last time I checked, is 506 people. That's including family reunions. Rumor has it that Mullen is where Kevin Costner filmed his Oscar-winning *Dances with Wolves*, but I'm not so sure that's just a rumor.

There's a great quote from Ben and Bill that from the 8,000 acres of land that ultimately became Sand Hills Golf Club, they discovered (discovered, not *built*) hundreds of golf holes, and, when the smoke cleared, selected the best eighteen and just let the grass grow in.

They didn't move very much dirt to make this track happen, and that is a beautiful thing.

Fortunately, a friend of my friend Steve owned and flew his own double-propped, pressurized airplane (think plane, not jet, with just enough room for four gents, accompanying sets of sticks, hanging clothes and toiletries, but no toilet per se, at least not like you have back home). Steve's friend Dan wanted to experience Sand Hills so bad he could taste it, like honeysuckle on the vine. And since I had the way to get us *in* there and he had the means to get us *out* there, a beautiful friendship was formed and we quickly took to the skies from Traverse City, Michigan, and headed west to Mullen, Nebraska.

After a few hours in the clouds, we touched the tarmac in a tiny airport in North Dakota to refuel (this plane sucked down gas like the drain in your tub), hit the skies again, and a few hours of dodging thunderheads later we landed in a remote place called North Platte, at a private airport maybe an hour south of Mullen, where Sand Hills members (there are less than 300 worldwide) park their private *jets*.

We grabbed our stuff, hopped in a rental, cruised down I-97, and followed the only directions they had given us: *When you see mile marker 55, make a left.* I think it's pretty darn cool that there is no sign for Sand Hills Golf Club at mile marker 55. (Sand Hills is ranked number 11 in the world and number 1 among modern golf courses in the United States, though that's not what makes her so special). When we made that left at mile marker 55, as far as the eyes could see there was nothing but sand, wheat grass, beef cattle (think bone-in Cowboy rib eye), and ranchers, ranchers who were waving at us like they hadn't seen another person in months. A mile later we saw a sign for Sand Hills, though it's not really a sign but a logo, like a metal ranch logo, with just an S and an H, no words. We turned in and a few miles later pulled up to the pro shop, where they took our clubs and belongings and put 'em on a golf cart, which was our cart for the entire time we were there. That's our mode of transportation to and fro, be it golf course, or restaurant, with the first destination being our cabin where we'd stay for the duration of our trip.

Our rental car was no longer needed.

The cabins at Sand Hills were sparse but somehow perfect in that way, with one big room with two full beds, a lone bathroom, and an open deck overlooking the rolling

Dismal River that is privy to a breathtaking star show the moment the sun and moon trade places.

Goes pretty darn great with a nice bottle of red, a couple Cuban cigars, and moments of reflection with one of your best friends in the world.

• • • •

After we checked in, we made a quick dash to the first tee, eager to get our taste of the mythical Sand Hills Golf Club. The feeling was a touch surreal, to wake up in my bed in Northern Michigan this morning just 7 hours ago—and now ready to tee off at Sand Hills this evening for a sunset round.

I know there is a better word for it, but all I can say right now is, "Wow!"

As we meandered through the wide open 18 that is Sand Hills Golf Club, I couldn't help but think that each hole was better than the last, with the last being in your top ten of all time. The 4th in our group, Dan's son-in-law Chris, turned to me and said, "Adam, this is like playing golf on the moon."

I couldn't have put it better myself.

At Sand Hills, it's very hard to get your distance from tee to green, unless you have a rangefinder. As far as the eye can see there is nothing but prairie grass and beef cattle, cows who don't seem the least bit interested in giving you the yardage to the flagstick as they graze and moo in your back swing. They're loud, too, like cicadas on a hot summer night.

As for judging distance, there are rocks that represent a buck fifty to the middle of the green, but that's about it. This place is as natural as it gets, and I love that about it, and so you channel your inner Ben Hogan and pray you pull the right club, using your eyes to gauge the distance and not some number on a sprinkler head.

Golf as it was meant to be.

It's interesting to note that there are only caddies at Sand Hills during the peak season, which was not when I visited, so there were no caddies available. In a town of maybe 500 people, these residents wear a lot of hats. The guy opening up the pro shop at the crack of dawn, selling you Titleist golf balls, SH logoed golf shirts, and brass ball markers with the wickedly cool rancher style logo that morning when he checked you in? Well, that same guy will be serving you cold beer and Spanish peanuts at the

The windswept, breathtaking beauty of Sand Hills Golf Club. Something to behold indeed, but only a small part of what makes her so darn special. (*Photo by Adam Ikamas*)

bar that evening. And the next day you'll see him cleaning the carts, giving new meaning to the phrase "Jack of all trades."

• • • •

After we finished up on 18, still trying to take it all in but knowing that's not possible (when is the last time you played golf without seeing a stitch of pavement, not to mention views like these?), we headed straight from the green to this beautiful restaurant right on premises where I cut into the absolute best filet mignon I have ever had in my life, and I am a meat lover from way back. It was succulent, with just the right amount of juice, not to mention fresh as a daisy, and cooked to indescribable perfection.

Our waiter joked that my filet was the catch of the day.

After a meal for the ages, Steve and I returned to our cabin and straight to the back deck overlooking the Dismal River. Over another beautiful bottle of red (an Alexander Valley cabernet, if memory serves), we listened to the rolling river and gazed out into an explosion of stars, solved all life's problems, and then hit the hay.

The next morning at breakfast, we sat down at our reserved table with reserved seats. (I still have the little card with my name printed on it.) There are only 20 cabins, so even if it's full there are only twenty foursomes on the property at any given time. That day, it looked like it's just us.

Just *us*. Think about that for a second.

With bellies full of sunny side up eggs and night-black coffee, we drove the dirt road mile to the first tee to play the first of what would be a 36-hole day. Adjacent to the box was a really cool starter's shack/halfway house dubbed Ben's Porch. There's a wraparound deck on which you could kick back and have a cold beer while overlooking the entire property, vast as it was. We could see the general manager/director of golf through the window of his glass office, just smiling and checking out the surroundings. There was no official starter, no ranger, and the GM walked out and said, "Off you go fellas. Hit 'em good," then gestured to the awaiting swath of endless grass, golf holes for days, wind-whipping flagsticks, and beef cattle.

Crenshaw and Core moved very little dirt to create Sand Hills Golf Club. They just brush-hogged the native vegetation, planted fescue right on top for the fairways and tee boxes, bent grass for the greens, and that's it. I'd never seen anything quite like it, and I'd been in the industry over twenty years.

And the design, my goodness. Every hole at Sand Hills seemed like it could be played a million different ways.

You could lay up, go long, try to drive the green, hit a 5-iron off the tee or a hybrid—there were just so many different options on each and every hole. It was truly a shot-maker's dream course.

After 18 indescribable holes of uphill, downhill, and side hill golf, we dropped into Ben's Porch for a quick lunch, which was a grilled and loaded cheeseburger the size of a Frisbee! We're told by the chef that when pro football great Peyton Manning played at Sand Hills, he ate *two* of these whoppers, then jumped back onto the first tee and

The unforgettable 8th tee marker at Sand Hills, carved out by hand and standing proud. The minimalist aspect of this place is what makes this track so maximum. (*Photo by Adam Ikamas*)

played another 18 holes. Peyton still holds the record, as far as I know. After all, it was all we could do to finish *one* of these ground beef mammoths.

Peyton can have that record.

• • • •

There is no doubt Sand Hills is as minimalist a golf club as you will ever find, from the sign to get you there, to the way the golf course was designed and built, to the way it's maintained, to the cottages where you lay your head at night, overlooking the rolling Dismal River under a blanket of endless stars. Nothing about Sand Hills is fancy or over the top, yet it's all perfect, exactly as it should be for a place like this. The golf journey of a lifetime—the leader in the clubhouse, as far as I'm concerned.

Sand Hills is not a private country club, stuffy and hoity-toity. And even though this magical place is one of the most exclusive golf clubs in the world, it is also the kind of place where you can put your cowboy boots up on the table and nobody's gonna yell at you.

I need to get me a pair.

Chapter 14

TURNBERRY GOLF CLUB

Edinburgh, Scotland

7,204 yards, and some 3,709 miles from
my computer

By 84-year-old legendary Ben Wright, who, in spite of
his many talents, is remarkably humble, so the author
will speak in his stead unless he tells me otherwise:
Y'all, Ben Wright is the greatest golf commentator to
ever call the game, hands down.

*Author's note: Scotland is the birthplace of the game
of golf, the very place where the placenta fell from the golfing
womb, spilling out hickory shafted rut irons, feathery golf balls,
and an unparalleled love for perhaps the craziest,
yet at the same time most sensical, life-reflecting game
ever created. Without Scotland, there would be nay golf,
American or otherwise.*

Ben's beautiful story is the bridge from the motherland to our land. I so wish you were hearing him telling it instead of me writing it. Ben has a voice like no other, baritone and booming, with the most wonderful English accent since Sir Lawrence Olivier.

Ok, Ben, take it away.

Thank you, Tripp.

The date is sometime in September of 1974, and I had just turned 42. My boss at *The Financial Times of London*, the pink newspaper of which I was the first golf correspondent, very much wanted me to go up to the Turnberry Golf Course in Scotland and play in a 36-hole event called the Texaco Cup, because obviously Texaco was one of the biggest advertisers in our newspaper.

Not many know that Turnberry's Ailsa Course was designed after the Second World War, because the original Turnberry golf course had been plowed up and turned into an active air base for coastal command. A very dear friend of mine, Jack Wood, who is sadly long dead, had actually been a trainee pilot there, and apparently far too many young men were killed at the air base during World War II because of the damn weather.

They crashed in unplayable *weather*.

That said, when the draw was published, the order of the day was 36 holes, in a better ball format between a pro golfer and one amateur, both playing off the championship tees, but with no handicap for the amateur—he played off scratch. I was very unimpressed, underwhelmed actually, when I drew Peter Tupling, a professional from Yorkshire who had been a Walker Cup player as an amateur, but hadn't had much success as a tournament-playing professional, though he eventually became, oddly enough, an extraordinarily well thought of teaching pro for professionals.

Anyhow, that's by the by.

As I mentioned, I was singularly unimpressed by my draw and, well, I was enjoying the company of an incredibly beautiful lady named Linzi (I was single at the time). In between marriages, as it were.

Linzi was a fashion model and just incredibly beautiful, and we drove to Turnberry from London in my brand new, E Type Jaguar, which was burgundy-colored with pearl-colored upholstery, and just an absolute joy to drive.

Upon arrival, Peter and I played a couple of practice rounds, and didn't do too badly at all as the weather was perfectly decent.

On the morning of the first round the weather started to get a little iffy, and by the end of the round it was downright unpleasant. Peter and I finished in the middle of the field, slightly up the middle maybe, but not really in contention. Therefore, I didn't think there was anything really to play for the next day, so I neglected to practice (normally when at Turnberry I sharpened my game on the par 3 course between the Ailsa Course and the hotel, which I must say I found to be a wonderful way to prepare to play the big course), and instead grudgingly dragged myself away from the hotel and my lovely companion the following morning, and by that time it had gotten very much downright unpleasant out. It was quite cold, with blinding squalls of rain, and winds gusting in excess of 30 miles an hour.

I was a reluctant competitor, to say the least.

As they say up in those parts, when you can see the Ailsa Craig, the enormous rock in the Firth of Clyde, the Firth of Clyde, which is a bird sanctuary, by the by . . . Well, when you can see the Ailsa Craig, as I could quite clearly as I reluctantly made my way to the first tee, it means that rain is coming.

If you can't, it means that it is already raining.

• • • •

Peter and I started our final round surprisingly well, with birdies on the first and third, though a bogey on the second, which would be our only dropped shot of the day. I could imagine we were making our way up the field a little bit, but still I didn't consider us likely winners, until Peter birdied the 14th hole. Now, we played real authentic alternate shot foursomes back then—Peter was driving the even holes and I was driving the odd holes. So when Peter birdied the 14th, I stepped onto the tee of the par 3 15th; I think it was playing about 215–220 into the absolute teeth of the wind. So I took a tremendous lunge with my driver and managed to almost hole the shot, which caused the few spectators (there were *quite* a few, actually, probably a couple hundred) to go haywire because the ball stopped literally two inches from the hole.

So, I birdied that obviously, and my partner, Mr. Tupling, birdied the 16th, a par 4, with a lovely second shot over a creek, which is called a burn over there. So now we suddenly could see that we just might be in with a chance.

Although in those days communications were rudimentary at best, and therefore we really didn't know what the heck was going on.

But anyhow, I stepped up on 17, the par 5 where Nick Price made his eagle to cement his victory in his British Open win some many years later. And I hit, in those days, my persimmon driver, which I remember was a Toney Penna, and I hit a very decent drive; I then hit a very decent 3-wood and a very decent 5-wood. (Untouched on the 17th were my Hogan Edge forged irons, designed for me personally by Mr. Hogan himself to suit my puny game, after conversation and a lovely lunch at Shady Oaks Country Club with Mr. Hogan and his brother Royal. This was followed by a quick but fearful visit to the practice tee with the great man himself, who told me to: "Relax, man, relax! I am not an ogre!")

It took me three full shots to reach the 17th green into the strengthening wind, into squalls of stinging rain that came horizontally, and I can honestly say you had to turn your eyes away because the rain would hurt your eyes like the dickens if you allowed it to get into them.

So anyhow, I got three shots to the green instead of Nick's two, but I made a twenty-footer for a birdie. And so now we had 4 birdies in a row, coming to the 18th, which was played in a right to left whaling gale by now, and my dear partner birdied the damn hole by hitting his approach inside 3 feet! And so we birdied the last five for a 61. Suddenly, you know, there was this hope. So we went into the clubhouse, with the weather getting worse and worse. And eventually, to cut a long and tedious story short, we were tied for the trophy, the Texaco Cup.

It was a bit funny, when the boss man in charge said to us: "Do you want to go to sudden death, or do you want a card count-back?" Well, Peter and I knew we would be very unlikely to lose a card count-back since we had birdied the last five holes. So we quickly said: "We're not going back out in *that* weather!"

Which was worsening badly by the minute, by the way.

And so it was decided on a card count-back, which we won readily and thereafter received the Texaco Cup. It was Peter's first prize money—probably 1,500 pounds, not a bad sum in those days.

To me, there is no better way of celebrating such a victory, than *celebrating!* And that I did, right royally. So, next morning, I was in poor condition as you might imagine, and facing the long, daunting drive back to London, albeit in this beautiful car.

When I got out to the car with my lovely companion, we found that some roofing tiles had been blown off the Turnberry Hotel, now the TRUMP Turnberry Hotel, and had severely damaged, although probably superficially, the hood, or bonnet, of my E-Type Jaguar. So I was incensed, and I went into the hotel and I was screaming blue murder about the bloody hotel falling apart and destroying my beautiful new car. And a gentleman, I believe his name was Frank Hole, who was the then-head of British Railways, British Transport as I believe it was called at the time, said to me, "Dear boy, just send me the bill." And to his eternal credit, Frank and British Railways paid for a brand new body shell for my E-Type.

Meanwhile, the Scotland weather had changed with the change of tide, which it very often does, and quite honestly, most of the times I've been in Turnberry at that time of year (September), it's been really violent, but of course three years later I attended and watched in its *entirety* the Dual in the Sun, between Nicklaus and Tom Watson in the '77 British Open, with the weather more the likes of sunny Florida than Scotland.

It can be beautiful there, but very much more often it can be tempestuous.

I remember the best round of golf, including the Watson and Nicklaus round, I ever saw was the 63 Greg Norman shot in similar weather to mine but in the 1986 Open, which Greg won at Turnberry. He shot 63 in upwards of 30-mile an hour winds with misting rain, and had three bogeys in that 63. *Three!*

I will never forget that, because it was as good a round of golf as I ever saw played, and I am 84 years old. But I digress.

That really is about it.

. . . .

The Legendary Ben Wright celebrating his storied career with a simple glass of champagne at home, brand unknown. (It was Dom Perignon for those taking notes. Stop taking notes.) (*Photo courtesy of Helen Wright*)

Final author's note: Actually, it's not.

After hearing and trying my best to transcribe the beguiling tale of Ben's greatest golf course experience, I couldn't help but ask the legendary golf commentator and analyst just exactly what was the most sage advice ever given to him over his storied and illustrious 50-year career? Us mere mortals have all received life-changing advice, though we may not have always taken it, and I wondered what was Ben's.

Without a moment's hesitation, Ben replied: "Knowing when to shut the hell up!"

And then Ben explained how.

"Tripp, the best advice ever given to me was from the great Henry Longhurst, my guide and mentor, on the evening after my first turn announcing at the 1973 Masters. This, shall we say, life lesson, took place at the bar in the Men's Grill at Augusta, over six quickly sipped drinks by Henry, each one of them at my expense.

"I had asked Henry to kindly critique my first day of announcing at the Masters, quite eager to hear what he would say, since I so valued his opinion. Keep in mind Henry and I grew up together, Henry being born in the county town of Bedford, me in the village of Woburn, England. Henry, being a bit older than me, and after many shared rounds of golf at the 9-hole golf club Aspley Guise & Woburn Sands, well, Henry had sort of taken me under his wing.

*"Well, after the sixth drink I asked Henry, 'When are you going to tell me how I did?'
and he said, with his index finger raised to the bartender, 'One more drink.' And so I bought
Henry his 7th drink and he says, 'Ok, now I'm ready. Ben, you were absolutely terrible. You
were appalling. You ran off at the mouth like a dripping tap.'*

*"I was a bit taken aback, because I thought I had done quite well. Then Henry says to
me, 'You really must have been very nervous.' Well, now I was quite angry, and I said, 'Yeah,
well, I bet you were too the first time you did this!' And Henry said, 'Of course I was, but
I had the good sense to stay quiet! And you went crazy, talking up a storm!'*

*"Then Henry took a big gulp from his glass of gin and soda and said, 'I'm going to give
you a piece of advice and if you'll accept it, it will likely further your mediocre career.'*

*"I said, 'OK, give it to me, Henry,' and he said, 'Ben, we are nothing but caption writers
in a picture business. And if you can't improve the quality of the pictures with your words,
keep your damn mouth shut.'*

*"So then I said to Henry, 'Well, why did you take so many drinks to tell me this awful
news?'*

"And Henry said, 'I thought I'd feel less pain when you smashed me in the mouth!'"

*"Well, there you have it, my man. The best advice I've ever been given. I have honestly
based my entire career thereafter on Henry's well-crafted words."*

Sage advice, indeed.

Chapter 15

AUGUSTA NATIONAL GOLF CLUB (PART II)

Augusta, Georgia

Magnolia Lane, 300 yards, and 1.2 miles from Calvert's Restaurant

By Haskell Toporek, a 7 handicap *on* the course and a plus 1 *off* the course . . . at least he hopes, as it relates to friends and family

Those who know me have often heard me say: "If Bobby Jones, Arnold Palmer, and Jack Nicklaus called me to make a fourth and I had the chance to play with my sons or sons-in-law at the same time, I'd tell that untouchable three-some thanks, but I have already arranged a game." As much golf as I have played, and as many wonderful courses as I have been fortunate enough to tee it up on, none can top four hours on the course with my family.

Just name the time and place, y'all, and Dad will be there.

Now as for my regular weekend foursome? Well, sometimes you just have to test that relationship. Allow me to explain.

It is the middle of May on a balmy Friday evening, 1985. I'm working in the yard, mowing, raking, and trimming—the usual; I'm just trying my best to get that honey-do-list item out of the way before tackling my Saturday and Sunday rounds at the club. It's not an atypical weekend at all. That is, until my lovely wife, Dale, comes outside with a quizzical look on her face and says, "Honey, stop what you are doing and call Mark Darnell. Immediately."

I look up, and with concern in my voice ask, "Is everything OK?"

Dale assures me all is fine. "Mark said he just needs to speak with you as soon as possible."

Oh, Lord. Doesn't sound like all is fine to me. Mark Darnell is the Head Golf Professional at West Lake Country Club, has been since its inception, and I am currently serving as President of said club, essentially playing the role of Mark's man Friday. *What could possibly be going on now? On a Friday night?*

I dial Mark's number.

The pro answers on the first ring and I quickly ask, "Hey, Mark. Haskell here. Is . . . is everything ok?"

Mark answers my question with a question: "Where are you playing tomorrow?"

"12:08 p.m., at West Lake. Why do you ask?"

Mark calmly says, "Wrong answer. Haskell, be at Gate #1 at 8:30 a.m. sharp." He hangs up without saying good-bye. No good-bye necessary.

Translation: We're playing the Augusta National!

Now for the "testing the regular foursome relationship" part.

I make the calls to each of the three gentlemen I normally play golf with on the weekends, trying my best (but failing) to qualm my excitement. "Look, I just got invited to play the National tomorrow morning and I'm calling you within minutes of accepting that invitation. I hope you understand."

I wish there was some way I could clean up their "good wishes" to me, but this story is supposed to be "G" rated, or at the very least "PG."

• • • •

I have been very fortunate to play Augusta National more than once before this hen's-teeth-rare invitation, and have been a Series Badge holder for over 50 years, but there is just something about driving down Magnolia Lane that puts a giant, hope-this-never-leaves kind of lump in your throat. To paraphrase a quote from the late, great, Champagne Tony Lema: "You take a right off Washington Road, and as soon as you get inside the gate, you start puking."

Magnolia Lane with the sun filtering down. There's no lane or passage in the world quite like it. (*Photo by Joe Bowden*)

Truer words have never been spoken.

To my blessed golfing credit, I have played Pebble Beach, Cyprus Point, The Royal and Ancient, Carnoustie, Ballybunion, Pine Valley, Pinehurst #2, Doral—a.k.a. The Blue Monster, Royal Troon, Kapalua, PGA West, Harbor Town, Los Angeles Country Club, Yeaman's Hall, Palmetto Golf Club, and the list goes on and on. But there is *nothing* like the ride down Magnolia Lane.

Goose bumps upon goose bumps.

But I digress.

As I head out the door the following morning, Dale says, a touch emphatically, "Haskell, remember we have to be at Calvert's at 7 p.m. sharp for Melinda's engagement party. Please, don't be late."

I look my darling wife straight in the eye and say, "Honey, Calvert's is hardly 5 minutes from Magnolia Lane. What are the chances of me teeing off at 9 a.m. and not being ready for a 7 p.m. dinner party?"

She repeats (and Lord, I love that woman!), "Honey, we have to be at Calvert's at 7 p.m."

A nod, a quick kiss on her beautiful cheek, and I'm off.

I have an engagement party of my own in Heaven!

• • • •

On the West practice tee of Augusta National, the four of us lovers of the game gather quietly, some more nervous than others. Our host is the Club Manager, joined by John Gibbs Sr. (a fellow West Lake Country Club member and dear friend) and Mark Darnell, the aforementioned head golf professional at West Lake. Balls in the air at 9 a.m. sharp. Four players, four caddies, who are traditionally donned in their white coveralls, sporting green, sweat-stained caps, and low-tread, white FootJoy sneakers. As per usual, whenever I get the once in a lifetime feeling of playing Augusta, I don't remember a single thing about the first 3 or 4 holes, try as I might to get comfortable in this ethereal stratosphere.

Been there, done that, but still I can hardly breathe!

Before I can wrap my head around the magnificence of the day, the clock strikes one and we are through, with another rare and magical day at Augusta in the books.

Time to go home! Or so I think.

As we are putting away our gloves and tees, zipping up our golf bags and this most memorable day, our host walks over and casually says, "Fellows, as you know, there's no one else here today but us, so the dining area is closed. I have made arrangements, however, for us to go over to Billy's house (the chief agronomist at Augusta, who lives on the grounds). His wife has a few cold cuts for us."

My, that is so nice! Only at Augusta!

It is now 2:00 p.m., and after a belly full of a perfect, after-a-round-of-golf-at-Augusta-National lunch, I push my chair away from the table and prepare to leave. Our host, with a sly grin on his face, queries: "Have any of you fellas ever played it 'back'?"

"Back" is where the Big Boys play during the Masters tournament, and the three of us quickly lean in and simultaneously shout, "No."

"Well, that settles it, boys. But let's take carts this time, so we can hit 'em and get 'em!"

I sneak a look at my watch . . . 2:30-3:30; 4:30-5:30 p.m. Hey, I can make this work. Plenty of wiggle room with Father Time. Eighteen more at Augusta, this time from the back tees?!

I tell our host, "I'm in!"

• • • •

Four players, one fore-caddy, and three golf carts later, and it's "Fooooore!" and we're off and running again!

I feel the need to mention here that the difference (then) from the back tees where the professionals play and the standard tees where the members play is absolutely *absurd*. The golf course plays at least six to seven shots harder from the back sticks. I cannot fathom what "back there" would be like today, ever since they "Tigerized" it!

Anyway, as we once again go to zip our bags and this most memorable day, it is now 6:10 p.m.—yes, I have been dutifully keeping track of time—when our fore-caddy walks by me, angles in, and whispers, "Mr. Toporek, just so you know, we're going to play the par 3 course."

I gulp and say, "How do *you* know? And why?"

"Mr. J. is down seven bucks, and he really doesn't like to lose, if you get me." The word "lose" is barely off his lips when I hear, "Hey, you guys want to make it a quinella? We've got plenty of time to play the Par 3 course. Keep the match rolling, you know, until we finally have a winner."

I thought we already had one—me—although the money has yet to change hands.

I look at my watch, again out of one eye, swallow hard, and somehow get out, "Uhhhhhh . . . yes, I'm in!"

Ouch, that hurt. I swear I felt a tiny stab in my side, just under the rib cage. Alright Dale, I know that was you. Darlin', love of my life, please give me a break.

Nine purposely butchered par 3 holes later, I make absolutely certain our host Jim wins his seven dollars back, quickly hug everyone, thank Jim profusely for a day I could never forget (and obviously haven't), and with my foot barely on the pedal, I toll slowly down the sad part of Magnolia Lane, the one that brings you back down to earth.

I remember thinking I would have given two thousand dollars to do again tomorrow what I just did today, though I am certain I would be outbid, probably tenfold!

Before affirmation that I wasn't going to have my pillow tossed into the front yard after an overextended day at Augusta National, I was wishing I was this chap serving up seafood. Excellent seafood, by the way. (*Photo by Tripp Bowden*)

• • • •

I get home in 4 minutes, very much liking my chances, beating my ride over to the course by *2 whole minutes*. How about that, Time Keeper!

Then I see a small, hand-written note on the dresser in our foyer that ominously reads: "I have no idea where *you* are, but *I* am at Calvert's."

Uh, oh.

But like most dutiful husbands, I swallow my panic, hurriedly shower, almost dry off, and shave—barely missing my right nostril. I quickly put on a coat and tie, not concerned one bit about them matching, and boom! I'm gone.

With all the mustered strength of Gulliver on his many travels, and with head held high and confidence low, I walk into Calvert's. For a moment I think there is a small fire, then I see from whence the smoke cometh: out of Dale's nostrils!

I walk up to her and attempt to offer my usual hello-my-dear kiss on the afore-mentioned beautiful cheek, but instead I get, softly, but with no uncertain terms in its meaning, "Where have you been?"

I look her straight in the eye (the very same one I looked into at 8:15 this morning) and say, "Darlin', love of my life, please let me tell you what I did today and I beg you not to take this memory away from me."

Dale (damn, I love that woman!), looks me in *my* eye and says, "Haskell, go get a scotch and soda."

What a day, but more importantly, what a wife!

I love you, Dale.

Chapter 16

BALLYNEAL GOLF CLUB

Holyoke, Colorado

7,147 yards

By Will Smith, co-founder of The Outpost Club—a national golf society with a rather incredible annual event schedule—and a sometimes helping hand in the construction of some rather spectacular golf courses, such as Ballyneal

The address for Ballyneal says it sits in Holyoke, Colorado, which is nowhere in the middle of nowhere.

I have special memories of rolling into this tiny Midwestern town in August of 2005—my thirtieth year of life, having spent quite a few of those thirty years playing in the dirt. But as I took stock of Holyoke's dead-flat, nondescript landscape,

I found myself seriously doubting all the wonderful things I'd been hearing from my fellow dirt-loving friends who'd been working on the construction of this brand new— and in their minds, *unparalleled*—Tom Doak-designed golf course.

Really? Unparalleled? Here?

With the terrain runway-flat and stretching out mile after slopeless mile in every direction, I was thinking maybe the boys had come to their assessment of this place after drinking a few too many "Born in the Rockies" beverages at the end of too many long days in the sun.

Summers in Colorado are a lot hotter than you think.

• • • •

Bright and early the next morning, I left the town of Holyoke and headed south in my borrowed, open-top '97 Jeep, deep blue and shiny, still skeptical of my buddies' declarations but in a fairly jovial mood after a good night's sleep under my belt.

As I drove along the highway, the early morning light began to reveal a small bump of land along the southeastern horizon, so I headed that direction thinking maybe, just maybe, there might be some interesting golf-ground along the way. After turning left onto one of the many dirt county roads that pepper this part of Colorado—they are seemingly everywhere, though road signs are few—that little bump in the earth began to rise out of the ground as if by some sort of Mother-Nature-sleight-of-hand, and a variety of shadows began to play upon its face.

I was intrigued.

But it is not until you turn to the south once more that the true potential of the tundra that becomes Ballyneal starts to reveal itself. The washboard road that I'm travelling on slinks around the edge of a massive dune that now rises almost 100 feet into the air. Now, *this* is what I had been hearing about.

This is ground for golf. Wow.

• • • •

The entrance to Ballyneal was and is still not very well marked (to this day, it is still very easy to blow right by it), but in my determined meanderings I somehow managed to find it. I followed the rising dirt road over what could only be described as a massive dune—where it came from I don't know—and rolled into the maintenance yard. With my ragtop in park, I met up with my good friend Don Placek, one of Doak's seriously talented design associates. With the maintenance yard quite isolated from the course and located in a low dip on the far side of a rather long ridge, the course itself was still a complete mystery to me.

After a quick "hello" we hopped into Don's Gator and set out to tour this mysterious Ballyneal golf course. After ascending one of many hills, I was finally able to get a great glimpse of just what the heck my intuitive friends had been up to, and man, was I blown away. The landscape was sprawling and surreal, and the course, as I was to learn after well over two lengthy stints helping put the finishing touches on the construction of this magical place, suited the land perfectly.

Ballyneal Golf Club—the name comes from the family that had the original vision to turn this tract of land into a golf course, the Neal family, and the Celtic descriptor Bally, which means "the place of"—is laid out over a vast swath of sandy dunes called Chop Hills, with the landscape much more abrupt than Coore & Crenshaw's iconic Sand Hills Golf Club, which is located maybe three hours northeast. Doak and his very talented cast of creators were able to route the Ballyneal course perfectly hither and yon, meandering as nature intended throughout the dunes to maximize a wide variety of tee boxes, holes, and green sites.

The fairways are Augusta-wide—come on and grip it and rip it, they beg you—but with heaving contours that demand you find the *absolute* right spot to which to rip it in order to have the best angle to attack a flag tucked behind a hollow or a knob, denying the arrival of your Titleist.

Ballyneal's blown-out style bunkers are often massive and foreboding, but they are also some of the most stunningly beautiful in all of the game. They appear to be naturally carved by the wind, and feature some seriously gnarly nooks and crannies, surrounded by native grasses, flowers, and yuccas. The greens here are in immaculate condition, requiring quite the imagination and the deftest of strokes. They often ask you to get creative, as the straight line could result in a putt that veers way *off* the line, but the smart player can use counter slopes to get the ball close to the hole, whatever the heck that means.

I have yet to meet that smart player.

And at the end of the day, as the sun sinks beyond the towering dunes, Ballyneal comes alive with thousands of sunlit dancing shadows. There just may not be a better spot to be in the world of golf than Ballyneal at sunset. If there is, I'd love to see it.

• • • •

I was able to discern some (and maybe most) of what I've just told you on my first tour of Ballyneal, and over the next month or so of helping to put the finishing touches on

One of many, seriously hilly slopes made not so much for the layout of this phenomenal golf course but to jump four-wheelers after a long day of working on developing this amazing track. (*Photo courtesy of Will Smith*)

the last few holes to be seeded, I really learned to appreciate it. But my many trips back to Ballyneal as a guest have taught me just how much fun this golf course is to play.

Not all great golf courses are.

From opening day, the culture of Ballyneal has been all about firm and fast conditions. Limited watering and the tight sand subsurface ensure that the ball is going to bounce—and I mean *bounce*. The tight fescue turf makes playing along the ground not only an option, but often the preferred method of attack, much like Old McDonald at Bandon Dunes (also one hell of a track, and a Doak-designed track, I might add). Think bump-and-run at Ballyneal, but with every club in your bag. Driver included.

Downwind in this neck of the woods, you may have to land your punch shot 8-iron thirty yards short of, say, the second green, and watch it run like a sewer rat up onto the putting surface. Fly it onto the green and it will bound into eternity.

• • • •

When reflecting upon my experience during that summer in Holyoke, Colorado, in '05, I can't help but believe that the biggest reason Ballyneal is such an absolute joy to play is that the people who designed it, built it, crafted it and cared for it had such a great, great time playing around in this giant sandbox of a sandbox. You can feel it in her bones, and so can she, crazy as that may sound. What a magical and special place to have the opportunity to create a golf course such as Ballyneal. Chance of a lifetime, truth be told.

One more thought, if I may.

I remember running into my good friend Kye Goalby that first sunrise morning while riding on the Gator, still not exactly sure what to think about all the accolades placed on this place. For the record, Kye shaped many of Ballyneal's bountiful bunkers and greens, is one of the absolute best in the business, and what a fool I was to ever doubt him.

Well, when Don and I rolled around to where Kye was working his magic, we could see that he was spinning around the green on a small machine that had a drag mat in the back and a miniature blade on the front, making small adjustments to the contours that were to be seeded the next day. He was so jazzed as to what was being sculpted. Kye knew that the boys were onto something pretty cool.

And I did, too, once I saw Kye in action.

Kye loves to tell the story of how more than just a few of the bounding fairway contours are the result of trying to make jumps for the four-wheelers that they used in the beginning to traverse the property. How cool is that? And the fun did not stop there when the guys and I left the grounds every evening to return to town, as the crew warmly embraced the local "culture," with frequent trips to the town's two main bars: Bilistie's (Bill & Kristie's) and KarDale's (Karen & Dale's). These places were just as you might wildly imagine for a rural farm community—think modern-day *Gunsmoke,* but not *too* modern and without the bullets—selling Coors by the case and featuring quite the cast of characters, all of whom were pretty darn welcoming to us interlopers.

To this day, I have never had more fun on a golf course construction job than I did that month and change I spent in Holyoke, Colorado, and I have done my share of course construction jobs, loving every single one of them. For those of you who venture out to that special spot in the Midwest, please don't get discouraged as you roll into that tiny Holyoke town—complete with its one stoplight. Just get yourself a good night's sleep at the local motel, turn your wheels south, and you'll find that one of the greatest golfing playgrounds in America lies just over the horizon.

Hit 'em good, and tell the GM, Dave Hensley, Will Smith sent 'ya.

Chapter 17

RANDOLPH COUNTRY CLUB

Cuthbert, Georgia

2,972 yards

By Tripp Bowden

Randolph Country Club is where I first broke 50 on nine holes, using every hammer in my bag. No easy task, when you're weighing about a buck-ten and your skill level bubble floats to the right and the left, and seldom ever in the middle.

I broke 50 at Randolph Country Club in beat-up Reebok high-tops and faded khaki shorts to earn my first ever pair of golf shoes: bright-white FootJoys, with mud flaps over the laces that touched the tippy-toe of the shoe (not a good look, looking back, but man, did I love those skips), and Tungsten spikes so sharp you could climb a mountain with 'em, assuming you would want to climb a mountain in golf shoes.

But at least you could climb the next hill.

FootJoys, given to me by a once-in-a-lifetime man by the name of Freddie Bennett, who humbly doubled as Caddy Master of Augusta National Golf Club for over 40 years,

until old age took over (well, not really—he was only 70—though mandatory retirement told him it was time for a change), and Freddie went on to other things.

It was a friendly wager between Freddie and me, especially since I had no horse in
the race, just myself, and my very limited level of skill.

"Break 50," said Freddie, "and I'll get you those FootJoys. Show me you're a real
golfer. Ain't no *clowns* out there breaking 50. Show me what's inside you, and I'll get
you those FootJoys."

Freddie made good on that bet, and so did I.

Randolph Country Club. The only thing country about this place is the surroundings,
not the name. Yet at the same time it's not exactly *in* the country, with wheat and corn
fields abounding, but way out to the left and the right. It's more like country come to town
(one of my grandma's favorite phrases, though I'm still not exactly sure what it means).

You wheel up to the course into a mostly empty (unless it's the weekend or 5
o'clock) parking lot, park your car on the left-hand side near a cloak of dogwoods, and
you're hardly three steps from the 1st tee box, a 90-yard (if that) downhill par 3 that
will eat your lunch and the sack it came in. But you don't know that yet. Right now,
you don't know anything. At the moment, this place looks like a chip-and-putt muni.
Leave your driver in the trunk. The long irons, too.

That would be a *really* big mistake.

It's the honor system here at Randolph, with a weathered brass tube thick as a double gumball and maybe a foot long, sitting crooked on a stand beside the first tee with
a note saying: *Pay Green Fees Here: $2.00.* At first glance, it seems overpriced, but you
slip your two Washington's into the barrel of the honor gun anyway.

The first hole at Randolph that will eat your lunch (curious—was it a sandwich or
salad?) is just like the other 8 (or make that 18, when you jump on the back tees at the
turn, the same place where you started) is surprisingly well-groomed, with everything
nipped and neatly tucked, including the old-school wire trash cans, where the trash
is exposed so the beer and soda cans that are half empty can pour out, and not in. So
Marvin can see what he's up against, I reckon, be it bees or yellow jackets.

Marvin is a one-man wrecking crew at Randolph Country Club. Cutting the fairways on a daily basis with a tractor designed for farms, not fairways, Marvin always

makes sure the entire place looks high and tight. The fairways, the bunkers, the greens, even the scrubby shrubs that cloister the clubhouse—was Marvin military? I don't know, because Marvin doesn't speak, but man, this place looks damn near perfect, even with the sunburn streaks on the fairways.

I am about to slide back in time.

Care to join me?

• • • •

I am a kid, age 11, and playing golf solo; no golf cart for me 'cause I am too young to drive a car, much less a cart, just the bag slung onto my left shoulder but I don't list, with my dog Geraldine right beside me, step for step. Geraldine is a wild mix of a dog who has been my absolute best friend since I was two years old. We were puppies together.

We're staying at my Grandma Memaw's house at 115 Taylor Street, in Cuthbert, Georgia, the small town where my mother grew up. Born just a stretch down the road in Cordele, she and my Aunt Andy called this place home until they left the nest at age 18.

Home is home, no matter where the heart is.

• • • •

Standing on the 9th tee, I see Marvin rolling down the hill on his big ol' farm tractor, making short work of the fairway's weeds and Bermuda, with the sun trying its best to slip behind the trees before Marvin can finish the job. You can guess who wins the race.

It ain't the sky.

Marvin sees me and stops his tractor. Without words or even a holler (his back is to me; how he saw me I'll never know), Marvin gestures for me to let it rip and I gesture back, *No, Marvin, I don't think I can hit it that far*, and Marvin gestures without words but a twirl of his arm, *Yeah, Kid, whose name I don't know, I bet you can!*

For reasons *I* don't know, I believe Marvin and rip it I do, right over Marvin's head, not by much but over just enough, and the ball bounds down the concrete-hard fairway, as does my dog, Geraldine, outrunning me to the finish line, where a 9-iron to six feet awaits.

Marvin doesn't turn around, just points a finger to the sky and rides off on his tractor.

This is what golf is all about, I think, in my small, 11-year-old brain that sometimes substitutes for a mind. A boy and his dog and Marvin on his tractor, waving us through while he's cutting an endless sea of fairways: *Come on and play, kid, and have fun*, says Marvin's index finger, pointing to the sky as if to say: *They say that's the limit, but you and I both know it ain't.*

Not even close. What I wouldn't give to get waved through one more time, but there's no time for that.

There is so much more to tell.

• • • •

There is the mythical Tom Lacy, the postman who moonlighted as the head pro of Randolph for over thirty years. Was Tom 60 or 70 when I first met him in my beat-up Reeboks and broken-down swing? It's hard to say, as Tom was ageless. He looked the same the first and last day I saw him, like Robert Redford, though not quite as handsome (after all, who is?).

Tom couldn't hit it from here to the cover of this book, but my goodness, could that man chip and putt! I have never seen someone so automatic, before or since. If Tom ever failed to get it up and down, I was not around to witness.

Tom was a damn good man, a kind and gentle soul who always let me have a game with him and his cronies: his favorites being a fellow named Bill Daniel, who always had an unlit cigar dangling from his chops; Lovett Geeslin; Bill Westbrook; and a curious gent named Mack Beard, who seldom said a word but wore a permanent smile on his face. I thought that the funniest thing about Tom's crew was that they all rode solo, enjoying the freedom, I guess, of having your own golf cart. I found that oddly funny. Still do.

Sadly, Tom is long gone, a ghost of Christmas past, rolling in putt after putt somewhere high up in the sky.

At least I hope so.

• • • •

When Father Time forced Tom Lacy into permanent retirement and then eventually a nursing home (so I heard), the guard changing was surprisingly smooth, with husband and wife retirees Harry and Ms. Betty taking over the wheel. Harry was quite the character, but with a nickname like Monkey Swing—given to him by the local kids, a name that was a rather accurate moniker for Harry's homemade golf swing—what else could he be?

Ms. Betty was quite the character, too, herself the proud owner of a hole-in-one on the aforementioned par 3 1st, ripping a beat-up, laminated driver off the box that never got off the ground, just bounded its way down the hill and straight through the front bunker before it arced like a diver and one-hopped into the cup, much to the chagrin of Sir Monkey Swing, who had never made an ace in all his days of trying.

Still hasn't, far as I know.

Ms. Betty could also grill a mean burger, and you could smell the grilled goodness soon as you walked up to the angled 9th green abutting the pro shop, the glorious smoke billowing from the grill and into the swirling south Georgia wind, your tummy rumbling with the thought of that first, drip-down-your-arm-juicy bite. And Ms. Betty's thirst-quenching lemonade defied description. The kids thought so, too.

My kids. With absolutely no clue what I was doing and armed only with my deep love for the game, I had started a junior golf program at good ol' Randolph Country Club back in the summer of '92. I was jobless at the time, as the golf course where I caddied for a living always closed down from the third week in May through the third week in October. It was (and still is) a rich man's golf course, make that a rich *northern* man's golf course, but "it's hotter than a snake's ass in a wagon rut" (man, I miss you, Robin Williams) in Augusta, Georgia during the summer, so I get it. Way too hot for rich folk to be out playing golf.

Poor folk, too, for that matter.

Most of my kids at Randolph had never even seen a golf club, much less ever played the game. They were Deep South, small-town kids, attracted like moths to a flame to sports like baseball, basketball, softball, and football, not chasing around a little white ball with dimples.

But man, did they ever get into it!

• • • •

At Randolph Country Club there is no practice facility as you and I have come to know, aside from her hard sloping putting green that's small enough to fit into the back of a truck bed, so the kids and I make one of our own.

Like a group of motley, modern-day pioneers, we carve our practice tee from a slab of earth between the 4th and 5th fairways, some 60 yards wide but nowhere near long and deep enough to pound the rock with the Big Stick. The earth here is hard-pan in the best of places, red rock-hard Georgia clay with spindly grass sparse and patchy, but it's great for learning how to play the game the right way—great for learning how to dig it out of the dirt.

Dig it out of the dirt. Is there any other way?

And dig it out of the dirt my kids do, some more so than others, but they all dig it out best they can, some to a surprising level of success.

The following summer ('93) one of my kids, an extremely athletic and gifted girl— less than 12 months removed from her first-ever encounter with a golf club—wins the women's club championship, following a roughed-up, first round 92 by fashioning a mighty fine 78 the following day in pretty damn tough conditions.

Can you imagine breaking 80—and in turn, taking home the title—less than a year after picking up a golf club at the age of 11?!

To take home the title, my stellar student clips the beastly much older Mona, she of the milk jug full of Bloody Mary's fame (Mona drinks one jug of Bloodys each 9 holes!), with a vicious hip kick and waggle that'll move Heaven and earth, both at the same time!

To make it all the more beautiful, my kid shoots 78 with *me* on the bag. Me, on the bag, because I heard through the grapevine that she shot 92 the first day, and even though she's only been playing golf less than a year, this kid ain't no 92 shooter.

• • • •

On the second day of the Club Championship, the back 9, number 11, my kid blows her approach over a baked-out green into an absolute mother of a lie: hard-pan for days, rocks all over the place, seemingly no way out. She looks at me, then at her wedge, then back at me, and I twist my face and shrug. This is her show, but my gut says she has the curtain call covered. I can't help but wonder how.

She reaches over to her golf bag and pulls out her putter.

Oh, did I mention she's a great putter?

Remember perfect practice from the Tupelo days? Well, she was like a kid in a candy shop with that modus operandi. This is also the same kid who would win the Naismith Award her senior year in high school for scoring over 2,000 hoops points in her career!

From eighty feet out, with the club championship outcome hanging like laundry on the line with a tornado coming, my kid calmly rolls her ball to an inch from the cup. Over rocks and hard-pan and leaves and a stick or two and random stuff I didn't kick out the way. One of the best shots I have ever seen in my life.

Before she walks up to the green to tap in for par, she stops and smiles and says to me with a finger pop on my chest, "Coach, that's called wanting it."

How good is that!

You know how I often say there is more, always more, especially when you know where to look?

Well, one of my kids from Randolph Country Club got a full-ride scholarship to the University of Georgia, with all the bells and whistles of big-time Division I college golf. She also became a three-time All America golfer, and even won her first collegiate tournament as a freshman.

But as a great man once told me: Tripp, I just opened the door. How you walk through it is up to you.

Sadly, relentless back troubles took this kid off the LPGA Tour almost as soon as she got there, but she stayed on track in the golf world and started her very own golf teaching facility in Atlanta, Georgia. But, once again, she is home, with all the bells and whistles.

Word on the street is she is very good at what she does.

I believe it.

• • • •

The last of my kids is my ultimate champion, but without the trophy.

I know I'm bouncing around, but let's back track, just a bit, if you don't mind, to Coach T's Open at Randolph Country Club, circa 1993. This kid is maybe 9 years old. Did I mention I think the world of him, and this moment in time broke my heart while at the same time made me admire this special kid all the more?

It's day two, the final round, and with the tournament in the bag and the zip strings about to zip it shut—he was leading by 6 shots at the time, if memory serves—

Me and my very youthful kids after the first Coach T's Open. I could not be more teary-eyed-proud of every one of them. (*Photo courtesy of Jo Hixon*)

he inexplicably dunks his third shot into the par 5 13th bunker, into a brutally nasty fried egg of a lie.

A fried egg like that at the Waffle House would sell for twice the price!

With no way out, and with no permission for me to lean in and give instruction or advice, just helplessly observe, this kid blades that ball out of the bunker, over the green, and into an absolute countrified jungle of trees and ivy and random shit.

I absolutely love this kid. I love his drive, his heart, his desire, and his genuine love for the game of golf. He has gotten under my skin (my grandmother's phrase for when someone gets next to you and you just can't let them go) during our two summers together—this summer being our second and I pray not our last. With tears in my eyes and bigger tears in his, I watch as he slashes his way backwards and forwards, forwards and back, to an 11.

An 11, on a par 5.

The ball even moves once on its own accord, when my kid grounds his club in the jungle during this 11. Two-stroke penalty. But this kid counts every single stroke, just like I taught him to—play by the rules or don't play at all. With torn admiration I watch as he counts backwards with a determined but shaking hand before penciling in an 11 on his sweat-soaked scorecard. He will go on to lose by 1.

A broken heart never felt more proud.

People often talk of the good 'ol days. Well, those actually were. Not in *spite* of that 11 my kid made, but *because* of it. That kid will go on to become one of the premier firefighters in America, often called upon to fight fires and save lives all across this great country of ours.

How good is that!

Thank you, to all my kids, for these memories for the nursing home.

Chapter 18

CYPRESS POINT CLUB

6,524 yards

Pebble Beach, California

By Tripp Bowden

O ur plane lands, but our luggage doesn't. Our golf clubs, thankfully, do. Welcome to Sunny California!

Except, well, it's not.

It is a quarter past midnight and dark outside as a beat-up banana, though I don't feel the toll of the late night hour. There is a three-hour difference between Georgia and Cali, and then there is the extra added adrenaline to know you are going to peg it up at a place called Cypress Point. Cypress is a club as much as it is a course, or so I am told. I only know through hearsay, though today I am about to hear it and say it for myself.

But right now I am as jazzed as Preservation Hall! Cypress Point. Am I really here? With my dad, my hero, and even myself?

I pinch my arm to make sure I'm not dreaming. I have my Ping sand wedge tucked in my bag beside my hotel bed, but I am still wearing the same underwear I slipped on this morning before I flew across America.

Who gives a damn about luggage when you're about to play legendary Cypress Point Club?

Cypress Point.

Taking Augusta National out of the equation, then Cypress holds the title of the most exclusive and difficult golf course to get onto in the United States, unless, of course, you are a member—though there ain't no slipping in sideways on Augusta either, these days.

Cypress Point is strictly members only. Of course, we are not members.

My dad and I are here via a courtesy call from one man to another, from the only man with phone call access to any golf course in America, as in *every single one of them.* I wish I could tell you his name, but the code of the road won't let me. But that's how these things work—trust me on this.

Cypress Point Club.

I say these words out loud, with my head on my Motel 6 pillow, and the words resonate, as if to float out in front of me, like a perfect puff of smoke from a Cuban cigar I've always dreamed of smoking but never could afford.

I'm playing golf at Cypress Point first thing in the morning, with my dad. Just a boy and his dad, playing golf alongside some of the most breathtaking coastline you will ever see.

I cannot ask God for a better day—better than the day flying over, nor better than the day that is to come. Damn lucky boy, me.

• • • •

The sun rises, as the sun is wont to do. But before we get out into the light, do you mind if I please back-pedal a bit?

It's the California airport, just shy of midnight.

Pop and I grab our clubs from baggage claim, looking around for our luggage on a carousal that slowly turns empty, with all other passengers gone. Pop gives the address of our hotel to a random and rather clueless attendant, who promises immediate delivery, as soon as our luggage arrives. But I couldn't care less about clothes or a toothbrush. I got my sticks, Pop has his, and we are playing Cypress Point tomorrow!

Make that today.

A rental car and motel room later, we call it a night. Pop flips off the light and closes the evening, which is now early morning, with his standard line, a line I cherish and grew up loving: "Good night, Tripper. Don't let the bed bugs bite." And then: "Get some sleep, Smoke. Big day tomorrow."

Boy, is it ever!

I know sleep won't come for me, not with what awaits, but that's just fine. So I lay there in our Motel 6 motel room and stare at the popcorn ceiling, trying to picture the best golf day ever.

The alarm sounds.

It's actually the phone in our room, a wake-up call from the front desk, yellow light flashing with me wondering why. Wake-up call? I don't need one—haven't slept a wink. But Pop has. He's been snoring like a wildebeest since his head hit the pillow (later in life, when I become a dad, I will also snore like said wildebeest). This may sound crazy, but Pop's snoring is a very comforting sound, at least to his only son, about to play Cypress come sunrise. I look over into the blackness of our room at the LED clock sitting on the table separating our beds. The clock reads 4:30 a.m.

Yowza! I can't wait to shower up and go. And then it hits me, soft, like a velvet hammer. We don't have a change of clothes. I re-examine my Skivvies, the same ones I flew across America with, and Pop and I laugh and make do.

A quick shower and we don last night's duds, drying our hair over the air conditioner unit, combing our red and blond locks, respectively, with fingers since we have no combs, leaning over and laughing all the more, trying our best to look presentable.

I walk over to the bathroom and look into the mirror, with hair all akimbo. I am unrecognizable, except for the undeniable I-cannot-believe-I-am-playing-Cypress-Point grin on my face.

I am digging the look, of my hair and disbelief.

• • • •

Our rental car still sitting in the darkness of the crack of California dawn is a short one, as is the ride to Cypress Point from our now departed Motel 6. In and out of narrow roads we go, through ageless Cypress trees that have been chased and shaped by the wind and sea, marbled with gnarly curves and towering canvases, starving for sunlight, yet standing strong against the elements. Kind of like me, when Pop and I pull into the parking lot of Cypress Point Club.

I get out of the rental, stretch, and look over my right shoulder, towards the direction of what I think is the Pacific Ocean, when the pro shows up on my left, as if dropped from the moon, which is still glowing in the California sky. Pop doesn't say a word. He doesn't have to.

This is mythical.

I can feel it, see it, even though it is dark as an abyss. I know without a shadow of a doubt we are the only ones here. Just Pop, the pro, me, and Sandy, our caddy for the day.

So it's two golf bags, with one caddy who is easily six-foot-five and aptly named, with his sandy blond locks flowing like a weeping willow over the collar of his faded t-shirt. This shirt has seen many miles, as has the owner. Sandy doesn't look old, more like wonderfully weathered—much like the Cypress trees that surround us. Oh, did I mention that no one is allowed to play Cypress Point unaccompanied by a member?

Looks like today you can.

The pro walks up and there are brief introductions, but again no last names. I feel like I am playing a bad guy in a really good movie.

"You fellas need anything from the pro shop?" He points an index finger at me. "You need a sweater, man. It's cold out." The pro then points at Pop. "You, too, Doc. Be right back."

He's right. I can see my breath, like mist. Funny—I hadn't noticed until now.

The assistant pro zips in and quickly out of the mostly dark pro shop and comes back with two really good-looking sweaters, one coal black and one snow white. He hands me the black one, Pop the white.

"You boys hit 'em good," he says, in a borderline whisper.

Why is he whispering, when there's no one here but us?

By the time I slip on my jet-black, cashmere (at least that's what the cloth feels like, soft as it is) Cypress Point Club sweater with the logo of the 16th green and take a deep breath of sweet, salty air, the pro is gone.

Where to, I don't know.

It's as if he disappeared.

Pop and I walk over to Sandy, who is standing casually beneath a gangly Cypress tree. "Sinewy" might be a better word for both the tree and six-foot-tall-and-change Sandy. Sandy starts chatting with my dad, quickly explaining the lay of the land for our day (or in our case, a couple hours and change) at Cypress Point in great detail, as if we are on a secret assignment.

In a way, I guess we are.

In what first appears to be a rather odd gesture, Sandy points up into the top of the gangly Cypress tree we're standing under, and off sail our golf bags, now slung up into the tree, sans clubs, balls, and everything else. Sandy smiles and stuffs our clubs and what not quickly into two tiny canvas bags that look more like what an archer would strap to his shoulder.

"Let's go, fellas," he says, simply.

Let's go where? I can't see past the tip of my nose!

Sandy points to the first tee. I can't see that either. The only reason I know is because he calls it by name. It's still just a little after 5 a.m., give or take a few ticks of my Swatch Watch. Pop looks at me and chuckles.

"Lead the way, Sandy."

A few steps later and we're standing on the revered first tee of Cypress Point Club, driver in hand, waiting for the sun to rise. And rise it does, to my pleasant surprise much sooner than later, especially considering it still feels like the middle of the night.

• • • •

I'm sure there are better words to describe a mid-October sunrise at Cypress Point, but right now I'll be damned if I can find them. Yellow butter dripping off popcorn?

I'm thinking those words must be hiding in my golf bag, not the one slung on Sandy's shoulder, but the one dangling from the tree behind us.

I watch, mesmerized, as the sun creeps up, out, and into the horizon, like a little boy sneaking up on his big sister, the edges of that glowing orb billowing in the distance like puffs of yellow smoke. That West coast rising sun seems so close I feel I could just reach out and touch it.

So I do.

Easing me out of my trance with his right arm angled across my shoulder like a stretched-out rifle, Sandy points his index finger at the jagged coastline of the first hole at Cypress and says, "Aim it just off the right edge, there, Tripp, and draw her back into the fairway. The wind's helping—can you feel it on your right cheek—so all you gotta do is swing. Best line in. You're a player, right? They told me you were—your dad, too."

I can't help but wonder: Who is *they*?

Though I feel like I am frozen in time, I manage to unfreeze and, taking Sandy's gutsy but sage advice, I rip my Titleist 8 out into the right edge of a rising, buttery sunrise, the ball drawing back into the dewy fairway. I wish I could say I saw it bounce, but I'd be lying. Sandy is suddenly right behind me, so close he could snatch me up and hurl me into the Pacific, new sweater and all.

"Man, that's perfect! Absolutely perfect," he says, with a slight sigh of relief resonating in his voice.

I know that sound well. (I'm a former caddy, remember?)

Pop fires next, a mighty solid click of stick and ball, and again Sandy follows with, "Perfect. Absolutely perfect! Boy, I got me some players today. We're gonna have us some fun!"

Two hundred fifty-plus yards later, both Pop's and my Titleists are lying, side by side, in the heart of the dew-covered fairway, awaiting their next assignment. You can see our footprints stamped out behind us on the yet-to-be-mowed fairways, as if we just trudged through a thin layer of liquid snow. There are no words from Sandy this time, just a beautiful shit-eating grin that says: *I told you boys the right edge of the sunrise was the right line!*

I look at Sandy and smile, and with no words of my own say: *I've got me a damn good caddy today.* Sandy hands me a 7-iron, hands Pop a 6, and with two more fortuitous swings of the sticks but no mention of yardage to the pin (no need—Sandy is so good he is immediately clubbing us), we are off and running!

When you love the game like Pop and I do, you remember every single shot you've hit along the way—the good, the bad, and even the ugly. But today, my round at Cypress is an absolute blur, with my only concrete memory being my near birdie on the 1st. I also recall almost writing my last will and testament in a wasteland of a bunker on the 5th—or was it the 6th?—where I slash away like Zorro until Sandy rushes over and says, "Oh, Tripp, the members of Cypress consider this bunker a free drop." Sandy reaches down like a ninja and snatches up my ball the way you might a $50 bill blowing wildly down the street, tossing it back onto the fairway.

"A free drop," I say, as much a question as a statement. The look on Sandy's face tells me all I need to know. I unquestionably let Sandy pick it up and sling it anyplace he deems viable.

My blur of a day doesn't become hi-resolution until Pop and I reach the 15th, a phenomenal par 3 (though that word doesn't do that hole complete justice—told you

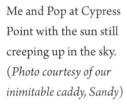

Me and Pop at Cypress Point with the sun still creeping up in the sky. (*Photo courtesy of our inimitable caddy, Sandy*)

I was at a loss for words on this one) that ambles along the Pacific coastline, the blue waves crashing on the rocks the only sound for miles, and the salt water almost splashing on your shoulders. Man, what a par 3, what a golf hole. As if God Himself had hand-carved it out of the Earth bit by bit, taking His big, beautiful hands and working unforgettable magic, saying, "Come on y'all, come and get me!"

No clue or memory of what I make there: a par, a 12? No care, either.

At this point, maybe an hour and change into the round, the only people we have seen for miles except for Sandy is a twosome with two caddies we saw at a crossway—members, obviously, catching the first light of the day that crawled into the sky behind us, probably thinking, if I were to guess, that surely Pop is now the newest member of Cypress Point. And with Pop's vibrant red hair and mine Motley Crue white, looking 8-ways disheveled and discombobulated, I am thinking those 70s-something members are also thinking: *What in the hell is this place coming to?*

I am wondering the same thing myself.

But there is not much time for dwelling on such matters, as we have arrived at the daunting 16th.

The 16th at Cypress—a par 3 for the ages! Sorry, number 12 at Augusta, I know you are special, but this baby is the granddaddy of them all—and I have played pretty much all of them in America, and even a little bit beyond.

There is *no* golf hole in America like the 16th at Cypress Point.

Stretching out into the Pacific like a dream of a girl you wish you would have walked up to in grade school and said hello to instead of good-bye, the 16th hole at Cypress is a hole like no other, with the Pacific Ocean curling up into her whispering hair. Yet you hardly know how to even say hello to her, in spite of your admiration.

My dad tees off first, with his driver, a persimmon head Wilson with a weathered face, from 217 yards out, into an absolute gale. It's Pop's best shot of the day, with the ball cresting into the wind and buffered beautifully by Cypress trees older than the Bible, protecting his ball as if God himself said to do so. Pop's ball lands some 20 feet from the pin—and then he maybe not so calmly cans it.

Son of a bitch! A birdie on the 16th at Cypress Point!

I have no memory of the 17th, perhaps because in my mind, I'm still at that 16th hole.

• • • •

The 18th hole at Cypress Point Golf Club is a rather curious golf hole. It's as if they ran out of room, or ideas. Or maybe golf in the 1890s was meant to be 17 holes, not 18. Either way, the 18th hole at Cypress doesn't make much sense to me, in spite of my love for this magical place. It's a very short par 4, with a hard dog-leg to the right. It's like raising your left hand in class to ask a question, and then the teacher tells you to raise your right, but still she doesn't answer.

Sandy says nothing on the tee, just hands me and Pop a long-iron and then a short-iron into the green. We take both as he heads on down the fairway. We love Sandy. He gets it.

Man, does he ever get it.

When we putt-out on 18, Sandy takes our blades and thanks us profusely for an awesome-ass day. Pop and I say the same thing back, but with different words (though Sandy said it best—it really was an awesome-ass day).

Wow.

With our clubs still slung over his broad shoulders, Sandy says, "Be right back," and he hustles over to where our empty golf bags are hanging in the gnarly Cypress tree, pulls them both down, and swaps out the goods.

The gnarly Cypress tree—we're right back where we started.

With our goods in place, Pop again thanks Sandy for a great day and slides two crisp Benjamins into his hand, much to Sandy's appreciative surprise.

"Wow, thanks, Doc. You didn't have to do that. This one was on me. I did this for Mr.—."

Pop interrupts with a finger to his lips. "I know you did, Sandy. Please tell him that Joe and Tripp said thank you very much."

Sandy hugs us both, slinging both arms around our backs. With one friendly slap on the shoulder, just like that Sandy is gone, waving good-bye without turning around—just a hand above his shoulder and a peace sign to the sky.

Sandy might be gone, but he is not forgotten. I can promise you that.

Chapter 19

ANY GOLF COURSE
IN AMERICA

104 Trillion Square Feet
of Coverage

By Zane Smith, current collegiate golfer
and chaser of PGA Tour dreams

When I was asked by the author Tripp Bowden when did I come to realize my rather unusual love for the game of golf, I thought: *Wow, what a question.* As for my answer? Tripp, I have no freaking clue. Or do I?

I may be only eighteen years old, and I may not know much for nothing, but I do know two things for sure. I am left-handed and am damn proud of it, and I cannot remember a day or time in my life when I did not yearn to have my hands cradled on a crooked stick so I could hit that little white ball as hard as I could into the distance.

And by day or time in my life, I mean since birth. Not sure why the left-handed thing matters, but it is somehow connected to my passion for golf.

More on that later.

When I was still in my mom's womb, my grandfather (I call him Papa) told my mom in no uncertain terms that he just knew I was going to be a boy, would be born left-handed, and that I would love the game of golf like none before me. How Papa knew that, I don't know, but Papa was completely right.

I got my first golf club on my first birthday—when I was barely even walking. It was plastic, and I wanted a real one, but still, it was my first club. After that, I can look at old pictures of me at age 2, 3, 4, 5, and so on, with a cut-down club in my hand, though these were now real, with steel shafts and forged heads. My Papa would literally cut down these clubs himself—by hand with no machines—in his workshop out back, and re-grip them just for me. Oh, the smile on his face and the mirrored one on mine when he handed them over.

I could be swinging that plastic club (and soon to be cut-down real golf club) around the house, or hitting orange golf balls during a rare southern snow fall (story to follow), but I always had a golf club in my hand growing up. And when I say always, I mean *always*. I drove my mom nuts with all the random golf balls lying around the house, hither and yon. Still do. Try sucking up one in a vacuum cleaner some time.

Makes for one hell of a racket!

• • • •

My mom likes to tell the story of she and I being in a K-Mart just outside Atlanta, Georgia, when I was only 2 years old. We were shopping for home goods, but I wanted to go straight to the toys aisle. As soon as Mom and I got there, I found exactly what I was looking for: a pink toy baby stroller.

Ignoring the color, Mom asked me why I wanted a baby stroller.

She said I looked her straight in the eye with all the seriousness of a surgeon and said, "To poosh awound my gawf cwubs."

Mom bought the pink stroller.

And sure as the world, that is exactly what I did. I pushed around my beloved golf clubs in that bright pink stroller. But Papa wasn't too fond of me pushing around my clubs in a stroller, pink or otherwise, so he did eventually buy me a golf bag. Papa was, and still is, the power behind my game—not just monetarily, of course, but emotionally, and in exponential, unexplainable ways.

• • • •

When I was not quite three years old it snowed at our home in central Georgia, and I mean a *lot*. Whenever it snowed in my home state it was quite the big deal, as most snowstorms in Georgia are 34 degrees of freezing rain, with icicles hanging from the gutters, melting and waiting to fall on your head, but this was a real and proper snow—fluffy and snowball-worthy. Yet while all the other kids were sledding down the hills in our neighborhood on pie pans and tinfoil, I was dragging around my cut-down golf club and hitting not a *white* but an *orange* golf ball, since, of course, one can't really

Zane: Me, hitting golf balls in the snow instead of going sledding with my friends. That's how much I madly loved the game. (*Photo courtesy of Papa Scoggins*)

see a white golf ball in the equally white snow. I chose the orange ball over the white one on my accord, at the age of not quite three.

I do remember it being a little tricky hitting that little orange sphere, since I was wearing layers upon layers upon layers of clothes and looking like the Pillsbury Dough Boy (tickle my stomach and make me laugh), much like Ralphie's little brother Randy in the classic holiday movie *A Christmas Story*.

It sure was fun.

Now that I think about it, almost all of the first memories of my life on this planet are about golf. There's even a photograph sitting on a bookshelf in our house of me golfing in that very same snow. That photograph has traveled with us every time we've moved, even all the way out to Phoenix, Arizona, where we currently call home.

• • • •

In the next year or so, I officially started going to a proper golf course, called the Trophy Club of Apalachee, a course that will always hold a special place in my heart.

Apalachee boasts tree-lined, narrow fairways, surrounded by houses big and small, but the dense trees make the houses feel as if they have disappeared into the wilderness, until you cross a street to play the next hole and realize you are actually in someone's backyard!

Any time I think of Apalachee, I think of my first par ever (on number 2, a short dogleg right par 4 up the hill with a long narrow green, and a sharp drop-off to the left, so steep that if you fell down it you wouldn't be coming back up anytime soon). I also remember my first ever birdie, on the third, a short par 3 with a narrow creek fronting the green, with a small pot-hole bunker guarding the middle of a kidney-shaped green just daring you to make birdie.

For the record, I chipped in from the edge of the green, so I guess it was also my first chip-in, too.

Apalachee was also the first place I ever broke 40 on 9 holes, as well as the first place I beat my Papa for the first time, many years later, at the age of 11. When I think about this course, I do not remember the holes, greens, fairways, sand traps, or tee boxes, per se—even though there are a plethora of memorable, weird, fun, and very tough spots on the track. I remember more the memories and emotions I poured out on each and every hole I've played since I was a little boy—the ups, the downs, and everywhere in between. Whenever I make it back to Georgia, I always make it a point to play Apalachee at least once; it helps me remember my roots in the game. (Just a note, I do remember every shot I have ever hit on any course. I don't forget *any* shot, good or bad. *Period.* That's how much I love the game.)

• • • •

I remember being just barely five years old, playing the game with my Papa and having the absolute times of our lives. We were, and still are, the absolute best of buddies.

On one cool, fall afternoon, after he picked me up from preschool, Papa and I walked into the pro shop to check in, just like we always did. I was *so* ready to go. I could not wait to play golf with my favorite person in the whole world.

The assistant pro behind the counter looked down at me and asked in all seriousness, "How old are you, son?"

With a smile on my face big as Texas, I proudly said, "I'm five, sir. Be six in January!"

I was thinking maybe they give you cupcakes on your birthday here?

The pro said sorry, but we could not play, since they had just (as in the very day before, according to the pro) declared a new club rule stating you must be at least six years old to go out on the golf course, even if accompanied by an adult. I will never forget the feeling. I thought the whole world was crashing down on me. I burst into inconsolable tears, utterly heartbroken.

How could I be that heartbroken at the age of five?

As I reflect back, perhaps it was at this moment I realized that the game of golf was my absolute life. I wanted so badly to go and play 9 holes with Papa, ride in a golf cart with his right arm draped around me like a favorite blanket, to be together and have one heck of a good time.

Just me and my Papa.

I didn't care what my score was, the numbers that added up to some sum at the end didn't matter a hill of beans to me. Even at that tender young age, I just knew I loved the feeling of the club hitting the ball, and the look of that ball flying through the air (even though it wasn't very far at that age), score be damned. But the best part of that whole explosive experience—the absolute very *best* part? Hearing the ball plop into the cup!

How's that for sounding crazy?

I didn't care if it plopped in for birdie or a quadruple bogey, but I knew I needed to hear that sound more often than not in my life. To this day, I still get chills up and down my spine when I make a putt with the distinct sound of the ball bouncing around to a stop inside the cup. Granted, I now prefer birdies, but the *sound* remains the same, just like the Led Zeppelin song from their classic album *Houses of the Holy.* For them, the *song* remains the same. I know it's a bit of a rather odd cacophony, the ball rattling into the hole with Jimmy Page rocking riffs on his Les Paul guitar, wailing away like a man possessed, but it works just fine for me. Does that make sense to you?

Probably not, but that's ok. I know I'm out there.

• • • •

Eventually, I made it to that coveted age of six. Not only was I now eligible to play at Apalachee again, but it was also that year that I sat in the den of my parents' house and saw Lefty for the first time. Lefty, the loose, left-handed free-swinging Phil Mickelson, up close and semi-personal on our big screen T.V., swashbuckling his way to victory in the 2004 Masters!

A left-hander winning a Major!

Witnessing Phil's never-say-die attitude and love for his fans and charisma on the golf course was so incredibly inspiring. It looked to me like Phil was out there having fun and just enjoying the moments, outcome be damned. Maybe it was because Phil was *left-handed* and he *won*, but I knew at that point, at the ripe old age of six, just barely able to read a full paragraph much less write one like this, that I wanted to be a professional golfer.

My left-handed self and my Papa (did I mention Papa is also left-handed?) played golf every week, religiously. I took some lessons, played in some tournaments, played for fun, played for keeps, played for my middle school golf team. Anything and everything

I could do in the realm of golf, I did. But my Papa was the golf connection in my life until my family moved from Georgia to Arizona. I was only 14.

Leaving Papa rocked my world.

Hell of a time to get lost and have to move cross country. I do like planes, but I like even more their return trip. This time there wasn't one. Saying goodbye to Papa and our times together on the golf course was the hardest thing I have ever done.

But, that is a different story for a different day.

. . . .

Once we arrived in Arizona, things changed dramatically. I was entering high school, and knew I had to be pretty darn good to make one of the best golf teams in America at Hamilton High School. Lots of really, and I mean really good players have gone to Hamilton. There have been six state championships (and Arizona is a big-ass state!), and more than just a few of the alumni—such as Andrew Yun and Richard Lee—have gone on to play on the European Tour and the Web.com Tour.

Even the bad players are pretty good at Hamilton. How could I *possibly* live up to those expectations?

At that point, I realized I was in a much bigger playing field than I was in Georgia. I had gone from sandlot ball to Yankee Stadium! So I sought out every resource I could find to get reconnected with golf, albeit on a level I wasn't familiar with, in my new home state of Arizona.

For the record, I got very connected, thanks to the help of some pretty special people.

. . . .

The first such person was the man, the myth, the legend, Eric Kulinna. Eric is the PGA Director of Player Development and director of the First Tee site at Lone Tree Golf Club, which is now my home course. Let me tell you, this guy really knows his stuff.

Eric is an intense, serious, golf-loving man who played golf at Penn State in the late eighties and if you have a question about anything golf, he is your guy. You take one look at Eric, and you know he means business. With his sharp jawline, jet black hair, thick raccoon-esque eyebrows, and deep brown eyes as intense as a football team before a rivalry game—eyes that will burn a hole through your soul if you aren't paying attention when you should be.

However, Eric is also like a pineapple, sharp and aggressive on the outside, but on the inside, full of love and sweetness. Eric is one of the most giving friends/mentors that I have to this day.

I swear to the Lord above with absolute grace, Eric is a walking, talking golf encyclopedia. I would take a solid bet Eric has never wasted a second of his life without being efficiently effective on God's green Earth, and I would not be where I am today without him.

I quickly learned, with Eric's guidance, that to have a great golf game, and by great I mean not just a skill set, you must not only play and practice every chance you get, but you must play and practice with the right mentality.

Eric taught me that competition is the best conduit for you to use while trying to better yourself at a game that is impossible to master. So I started to practice with purpose, trying my damndest to not waste a minute, even though I did, from time to time, being young, stupid, and full of myself, like the day I spent hours upon hours trying to hit trick shots and mostly failed. What the hell was I thinking?

I guess I wasn't.

• • • •

Eric helped me get ready for my first full-fledged golf tournament in Arizona, scared to death as I was, just 14 years old and a stranger in a strange land. It was the show-me-what-you're-made-of Winter Classic, held by the J.G.A.A. (Junior Golf Association of Arizona). I do not think I have ever been more nervous standing on a tee box in my whole life. I had never played in an event that seemed so, for lack of a better word (or maybe it's the right word), *large*.

I felt like my golf world had just been super-sized!

• • • •

Your first tee shot in a big-time golf tournament is kind of like your first kiss. You're nervous through the whole date (the warming up to said kiss), but as you get closer to the time and you feel it coming to fruition, you get anxious, and a touch goofy—heck, a lot goofy. As you hit the tee shot, or kiss the girl, all you can think of is *oh no*, but then as the ball flies through the air and lands miraculously in the fairway, and as you are trying to figure out what the heck to do with your lips, her lips, and you, and your hands and her hands, too, suddenly it's over.

Or has it just begun?

Still, you think and may or may not say, "Well, dang, it could have been a lot worse. Oh, and by the way, I hope this doesn't scare you away, but I think I love you."

And then you reach over to kiss her again, only to realize she's halfway home, riding shotgun in her best friend's car. With sincere apologies to the first girl I ever kissed (name withheld to protect the innocent), I hope that analogy comes across the right way.

• • • •

Back to the tournament.

At the time, considering the wind, rain, and cold (which was *crazy* weather for Arizona, where it never rains and is never cold), I played fine as frog hair, *excluding* the 9 I took on a par 5 the second day. I shot 76-81 to finish 9th out of 20 players. My first introduction to true competitive tournament golf at its finest, and I passed the test. The flying colors weren't there, but the passing grade was. Good enough for me.

That tournament was also the first time I met my new archenemy of the game I so very much loved: the pain and the art of falling apart and losing.

They say there is an art to everything.

I have played in many tournaments that fell apart right beneath my feet, shattering into shards, like a perfectly good crystal vase full of candy red roses, bumped unexpectedly to the ground. The pain might have hurt like hell, but I still knew that if I had a choice of being there or anywhere else, 100 out of 100 times I would still choose to be out there on that golf course, score or outcome be damned.

• • • •

Over the course of the next two years, every tournament round happened the same way for me. I would start off ok, but then by the 10th or 12th hole, I would find a way to mess up to the point of no recovery. I dredged through round after round after round. That said, not once did I give up my spirit and love for the game. I would always leave the course knowing I would not have rather spent those last five hours anywhere else.

During my junior year in high school, I started to gain a little momentum, putting a few really good rounds together, back-to-back and in proper tournaments, garnering a few top ten finishes in J.G.A.A. events. The only problem was my high school team, which was insanely stacked with talent (so much so we blew the field away at State, a 36-hole event we won by 10 strokes). I made the team, yes, but our starting five that year consisted of one guy who turned pro, three guys who went on to play college golf (at ASU, Drake, and Chandler College, respectively), and the other fellow who opted to *not* play college golf (even though he more than had the talent) but instead attend UC Berkeley, to get a proper education.

Needless to say, I did not play much on the five-man traveling team that year, even though I felt I had the game to compete with any player in the state.

I went guns blazing into my senior year of high school, in spite of having a fairly bad summer (not what I needed, as I wanted to impress the colleges for which I was hoping to play), with many tournaments just simply not turning out how I wanted them to, in spite of efforts to the contrary.

I played my way into a few fairly important tournaments, but seemed to have dismal rounds once I achieved my goal of reaching the championship tournaments. I cannot stress enough that my passion and love of the game never left. I never once doubted what I wanted to do. I knew if I bore down and grinded through the hard times, the results I wanted would finally come.

But still . . . the frustration hung over me like a cloud, and I don't mean a fluffy white one.

In any case, we had a brand new starting five my senior year, which included yours truly. Our season was much like my normal golf game, except now we did it as a *team*. We all loved the game equally, we were all hungry to win, and most importantly we just simply enjoyed the game of golf as it was meant to be. We came in second more times than I can count that season, but that's ok.

Second beats the heck out of third.

Finally, at the State Championship in late November, we played quite well, but unfortunately not well enough to take home a championship. Still, it was one of the most enjoyable weeks of golf I've ever experienced. I tried to soak up every moment of my final two rounds of high school golf, knowing very well the end was near, and holding on to every moment like a bandit in *A Fist Full of Dollars*.

I personally shot 75-76—not ideal, but still I so enjoyed the same game aspects of the game that I've grown to love since I picked up that very first club. While I wanted to win it all so bad I could taste it, sweat it, bleed into it, it also showed me—with all due respect to the great Vince Lombardi—that sure, winning isn't everything, but it isn't the only thing, either.

Sorry, Coach.

• • • •

After the season finished, I continued to play in tournaments. The most exciting and best weekend of golf I've played happened in the month of January 2016, at the brand new Grand Canyon University Golf Course. The yet to be finished clubhouse juts straight out into the air, with sharp edges and points on the roof, with brown and red rock siding, replicating the Grand Canyon, or as well as you can if you are trying to replicate such. Not an easy task, considering the Grand Canyon is more than 5,000 feet deep and equally wide, and one of, if not *the* most beautiful desert scenery in the world.

I was tied for the lead after the first day at Grand Canyon, in spite of playing a rather mundane round, never really screwing up, just enjoying a day on the course. I shot two over, due to the golf course being hard, firm, fast, tree-lined, and with rough thicker than week-old cotton candy. The second day a player in my group and I went back and forth, forth and back all round long. I made birdie on five; he made birdie on six. He made birdie on twelve; I made one on thirteen. Then he made a long, slippery putt on seventeen to go one up going into the final hole. I thought to myself, *this cat can flat out play!*

On the 18th, my opponent and I both hit gorgeous drives. I was away, and hit a pitching wedge from 148 yards out to 35 feet, not so good (I truly thought I was done for), then he air-mailed the green. Thinking he was deader than disco, my opponent hit a beautiful though improbable—no, make that impossible—chip to a foot and tapped in for par, leaving me shaking my head in a juxtaposition of disbelief and admiration. Talk about one hell of an up and down. I knew I had to make my putt to tie to hopefully force a playoff. Well, guess what?

I drained the putt.

I drained the dad-gummed putt!

I cannot describe the feeling that washed over me when I made that slow, curling, right-to-left, thirty-five-foot slow roller down the sloping 18th green at Grand Canyon. I had never been clutch in my whole life, until now. It was a rather odd feeling, and I couldn't help but wish for a mirror to see if I was really me.

My opponent and I walked to the scoring table, prepared for a playoff—I think I would love a playoff if ever I could get into one. But as my usual, unfortunate luck—not sure why luck and I have yet to become friends—some kid from Sandra Day O'Connor High School shot 66 to come out of nowhere and win by 1, which was an absolute phenomenal score on that golf course.

I ended up in 2nd place, again.

Damn.

That day at the brand new Grand Canyon University Golf Course continued my trend of crazy close calls, and sometimes they ring in my sleep (sometimes I answer). However, during that round and even after the round, I honestly never felt bad about it, knowing I poured my absolute heart into my game and played to the best of my abilities during those three insanely competitive days.

A wise man once said, "If you leave it all on the table, there is nothing left to sweep up." That wise man was my Papa.

• • • •

Soon after the tourney at Grand Canyon, I signed with fairly local (hardly 20 minutes from our house), Mesa College, one of the top five community colleges in the nation should you fancy a proper education. I received a partial scholarship, but a scholarship nonetheless.

After signing the dotted line, I continued to play all summer before enrollment—playing fairly well, quite well actually, shooting my best round ever in my last tournament as a junior golfer—67-72, as well as a 64—and also carving out a couple top 3's in some rather significant golf tournaments.

Perhaps the corner has been turned.

I try to live (difficult as it can be sometimes) what sports psychologist and mastermind Bob Rotella preaches day in and day out: "God has guaranteed you a win in your life, but you do not know when it will come. Therefore, you must prepare as if every tournament will be the one, and you must never forget the love that pushes *yourself*."

Pretty profound stuff.

• • • •

As of this writing, we just finished the fall golf season at Mesa. I played in the starting five in all of the tournaments thus far, methodically getting better than I was before—not great, no records set just yet, but better, still enjoying every moment of practicing and playing the game I love more than life itself.

It's ok to say that, right? I don't have a family of my own yet, no wife and kids—they of course would *be* my life.

• • • •

This may not be the typical golf success story, may not even be a success story at all, because, frankly, I have not had the breakthrough I have always hoped to have. However, I will never give up, I will never stop.

I won't lie. It can be damn tough, and I mean really damn tough, to never let doubt creep into my mind with all the chips on the line. But if and when that happens, all I have to do is think back to playing the game with my Papa, enjoying every moment together on the course, with Papa by my side.

Chapter 20

OCEAN POINT GOLF CLUB

Fripp Island, South Carolina

6,876 yards

By Tripp Bowden

There is nothing quite like the Low Country.

There is nothing like its comforting coastal breezes, the sensual smell of the sea, and season-long sunsets that never seem to end, with the sky the color of every crayon in Crayola's box.

Tucked like a pocket square at the end of U.S. Highway 17 lies one of the Low Country's best jewels—Fripp Island, a barrier slip of land dangling along the Carolina coast, first developed back in the 1960s, only to go bankrupt not once, but twice. That is insanely hard to believe these days, seeing as how Fripp has become a booming, family-friendly resort with yearly revenues in the multi-millions.

My, how times have changed.

These days, Fripp shines like the Hope Diamond when you are there with family and friends, with the island hopping like a bunny pretty much 24-7.

Freddie Bennett, the legendary Augusta National caddy master who you've met a few times on this journey through the soul of American golf, grew up just down the Intracoastal Waterway from Fripp Island, in the sleepy little town of Frogmore. The town may be sleepy, but it is also famous worldwide for their signature Frogmore Stew, an eclectic blend of shrimp, crab, kielbasa, corn on the cob, a mix of sweet and red onions, new potatoes, and whatever seasonings you've got in the cupboard that make your taste buds smile. Frogmore Stew.

My absolute favorite meal.

Long before Fripp was developed, Freddie and his daddy would take their John boat across the inlet to the island, where they would spend the day hunting wild boar and deer (did you know deer could swim?) that roamed the island's thick vegetation. Those wild boar and deer were dinner on the Bennett family table as often as shrimp, fish, or crab.

Looking at the pristine fairways and greens, well-sculpted creeks and marshes that shape and define the mighty fine test of golf that is Ocean Point Golf Club, that thought seems *very* hard to believe. Wild boar with tusks that can gore you? Here, on Fripp Island?

Built in the late sixties by mastermind golf course architect George Cobb, Ocean Point Golf Links is a test for the ages, regardless of skill level or the tees you choose to play. The head pro at the time of this story is a fellow from Michigan named Bill, with whom I quickly become dear friends.

• • • •

Our tee time is 10:45 a.m., and we are locked and stocked with our golf carts loaded down with a plethora of shit, from bags of boiled peanuts and ziplocs of beef jerky—no hot dogs at the turn for you cats—to boxes of stogies and the odd pack of Marlboro Lights—in the box, so they don't get squished—and a wind-proof lighter that wouldn't blow out in a hurricane, to nicely round out the necessary accoutrements.

It is quite the collection of shit.

Bill looks the other way when he's behind the counter of his well-stocked pro shop (Bill is a Hogan man, and the Wee Iceman's paraphernalia is everywhere, which is very cool, I might add), swiping your group's mostly maxed-out credit cards but charging only for the golf cart ($12) and not the green fee ($75), knowing damn good and well your college-kid asses can't afford it.

Bill's right.

Bill and I exchange handshakes and hugs and the boys and I head out to the first tee, a brutal par 4 with water hugging both sides of the fairway like a scorned lover that will never let go. I dream of an even par round and winning bets that run the gamut of crazy, such as the Dead Sea Par, when I make par after knocking my ball into the water; a Lewis & Clark, making par without ever hitting the fairway; a Trapper John, M.D., making par out of the sand trap; an Oozler, hitting a par 3 in regulation and then two-putting; and then there is the dreaded *reverse* Oozler, hitting said par 3 and then three-putting!

The list goes on and on.

Shooting even par on Ocean Point Golf Club, even though I am a fairly legitimate Division I collegiate golfer? Not happening. Not at Ocean Point, the birthplace of out of bounds. There are more white stakes out here than at The Home Depot!

Here, the term *re-tee* is a term of endearment.

Between my buddies and I, there are more balls flying out of bounds with nerves jangling and the wind howling like Wolfman Jack, you would think they're piloted by Kamikazes, hell-bent for the other side of those dreaded white O.B. stakes.

Ah, the days at Ocean Point.

• • • •

There are so many memories of Ocean Point Golf Club, but here is one of my absolute favorites.

It's an eighteen-hole match with one of my best friends, a brother I never had but a brother nonetheless, from the moment we met in the 8th grade on the school bus to Tutt Junior High, grinding it out hole for hole like Watson and Nicklaus in *The Dual in the Sun,* except he is Watson and you are Nicklaus. Skill set vs. skilled experience. There is quite a difference between the two, though today you are unable to prove it.

If it were boxing, it would be Foreman vs. Ali.

Yes, this is me, and my dear friend Billy D, a.k.a. Sport Billy. He is one hell of a player, a crazy gifted athlete, but at this point in time, circa 1993, he has yet to beat me on the links, especially not on the links of Ocean Point Golf Club.

Turns out it is one unexpected bear of a match!

Having started our round on the 10th, the 9th hole at Ocean Point is our last. Four-plus hours of battling howling winds, each other, and enough O.B. stakes to build the White House with no paint necessary, throw in creeks, ponds, and miles and miles of the ball-hungry Atlantic Ocean, Billy D and I stand on the final tee at Ocean Point all square.

After all that back and forth we are dead-ass even. Billy D is playing the round of his young golfing life, and I am struggling like a fly in a web with the Black Widow honing in, using every trick in my bag just to keep it between the navigational beacons!

Standing on the 9th tee, we stripe a pair of drives, both balls center-cut. Billy D is away, but the howling Fripp Island wind blows his little white orb over the waist-high, white picket fence that borders the ocean side of the green. Over that picket fence are mounds of sea grass; beyond that are boulders big as your car and waves that will crash you to the ground.

It is also out of bounds.

But I've had enough O.B. stakes for one day, so I say nothing. I'm quite the traditionalist, so I am a bit surprised when my brain tells me: It's your match, Tripp, it's your rules. If Billy D can find it, then by God, let him play it.

And so I do.

In spite of the same howling coastal wind that blew his ball over the picket fence and mine under the lip of the greenside bunker, I let Billy D play it. While he's hunting for his biscuit, I dig mine out to just shy of 10 feet.

"Can I mark it?" I hear him holler. "I found it!"

But he's got a question for me. He knows I know the rules of golf like nobody's business.

I walk over and see Billy D's ball nestled neatly in the sea oats, a few inches above the ground. It's not as bad of a lie as I thought—he can get a bat on it if he goes after it with the left wrist leading the way and no supination. I look him in the eye and ask, "So what's your question?"

He gestures with an angled finger and asks, "Can I see if the ball is small enough to fit through the gaps?" He points to the picket fence, which, as I mentioned, is out of bounds, but he doesn't know that, and I'm not going to tell him. I've already bent one rule. Don't see the harm in having a taffy-pull with another.

"I'll put it back in the exact same place, the exact same lie," he says. "But I don't want to break any rules."

Rules? What rules? As long as we play by the same ones, the playing field stays level.

Well, this time we are playing by mine.

"Sure," I say. "Go for it. I am curious my damn-self to see if you can pull it off."

Billy D is way too close to the fence to lob it over, so the only option is to go *through* it. The shortest distance between two points is a straight line, or so they say.

Billy D carefully picks up his Titleist 2 with the wavy blue, handwritten B over the number, takes one step forward, and slides it through the gap in the picket fence, the ball barely sliding through. I'm talking minuscule room on either side—enough for an index card, maybe, or the eye of a needle.

I'm also thinking that there's no way in the bowels of Hell can Billy D pitch that ball through that tiny-ass gap. This matchup is mine for the taking. I got you, mother-scratcher!

Without fully realizing it, I had just gone against my most important golf, and life, mantra: Always expect your opponent to make it, to make the next shot, the next putt—the next whatever, no *matter* the circumstances.

I mark my ball, with Billy D knee-deep in the fenced-out shit.

I step away and watch a miracle in the making. As if his golf ball has eyes, my dear friend pitches his ball through that tiny-ass gap as if he were pitching it through the Holland Tunnel! It lands on the fringe, bounces twice, and rolls within inches of the cup. A gimmie 4!

Son-of-a-bitch!

"Wow," I say, though the word "Wow" doesn't begin to describe what I've just witnessed. "Hell of a shot—one for the ages. You can pick that up, my brother."

Scene of the crime. Me and Billy D, not long after he finally pinned my ears back at Ocean Point, after many years of trying.

Billy D looks at me with a serious but goofy grin and says, "Can I finish it? Bottom of the hole, right? No matter what?"

That simple statement tells me Billy D gets it, and so I nod and say, "Sure. Of course you can."

He taps it in. Par. You can probably guess what happens next.

Just knowing I would make it, I slide my four-footer over the right edge of the hole and just like that, the match is over.

Damn. As competitive as I am, even when my A game is a low B-minus, I am very much OK with this ass-whooping. Billy D is a tremendous athlete, can play quite well every sport you can name, and he just hit the golf shot of the century. He was gonna beat me eventually—it was not a matter of if, but when. For the first time in my life, I got to determine the when.

Take *that*, Rule Book.

Losing never felt so good.

Chapter 21
THE CABBAGE PATCH

Augusta, Georgia

6,247 yards

By Tripp Bowden

The road to the Cabbage Patch is a curious one.

Depending on the direction, you meander past gas stations and quickie marts; a private Catholic School whose kids' parents have more money than sense; a Korean grocery store that—rumor has it—whatever they catch in the net that day they sell, and I don't just mean fish; the small local airport for private planes and medical helicopters; an oral surgery office where they can rip your mouth a new one; and the VFW, Local 2534.

This road is Highland Avenue, called thus because back in the day, and by that day I mean the 1800s, not the 1980s, this area was the highest point in Augusta, Georgia. The rich folk moved up here from down by the Savannah River, due to mosquitoes and flooding.

They're still here—the rich folk *and* the mosquitoes. Not sure the mosquitoes ever left.

Come in from south-bound Damascus Road, and it is altogether different. You will pass a deep blue, cinder block building on your right that moonlights as a speakeasy, as you drive through a rough and tumble neighborhood that prays for daybreak, and a can't-wait-for-sunrise old man who sits on the back of his beat up truck's tailgate, selling whatever vegetables are in season at a fraction of the grocery price. These are damn good groceries. Beats the hell out of what they're selling at Publix.

The head pro at the Patch is Mr. Red Douglas. All the folks call him Red for his hair color, and you will never really know his real name. He's as kind a man as you'll ever know, loves everybody and everybody loves him; imagine Santa Claus sans the beard, but with thin straight hair the color of a red, electric magic marker, if a magic marker could ever be electric and red.

As a kid, I never knew what the actual green fee was. Still don't. Mr. Red would just ask you what you had in your pockets that day: "What kinda jingle you got in there, son? A quarter, nickel, a dollar, a goose-egg? Lint?"

Mr. Red was usually right about the latter, but every now and again I had a few coins bumping around in my pocket, of which I eagerly handed over for the chance to put a peg in the ground at the Patch and see what I had in me that day.

Lunch at the turn was homemade chili topped onto the best tasting hot dog in Augusta, dipped up and served steamy and squishy by Mr. Red's wife, Ms. Anne, who always smelled like whatever flower was blooming in season. She had a beauty that was touchable (how rare and cool was that?), and she loved you like you were her own.

Mr. Red pats you on the shoulder, points you to the first tee, and tells you to "Hit 'em good, son. Find every fairway you can."

At first glance you wouldn't say the Cabbage Patch looks like much. The tee boxes are badly in need of grass and the world's biggest glass of water. The fairways are hard as marbles, and much like the game, and if you play here enough that's what those buggers remind you of.

You never get the same bounce twice.

But that only adds to the charm, as no two holes are even remotely alike. When you play the Patch you feel as if you just played eighteen different courses, not holes, with the first at the Cabbage Patch being a great example of the idiosyncrasies of this magical local muni. The first hole boasts an unhittable fairway, angled hard from right to left, like a protractor sliding off your third grade desk.

If a fairway could be an embankment, this would be it.

There is a drainage ditch that runs the length of this beast of an opening par 5, literally from tee to green. The drainage ditch, barely wide as an Igloo fishing cooler, guards an access road, in the way a moat might guard a castle. Like the ditch, that access road also runs tee to green.

It is also out of bounds.

And even though I have stood on that first tee box a thousand times over the course of my 49 years of life, knowing damn good and well that damn fairway lists like a sinking ship with cargo sliding in the hull, and the drainage ditch is more like a sling shot than a moat, my Titleist Acushnets, 384s, ProVIs, and ProV1Xs have all bounced onto that damn access road countless times more than they have fallen into the cup for a birdie. Or a par, or even a bogey on that postage stamp of a green, guarded by a pot bunker that makes the infamous Devil's Asshole look like a dimple on George Clooney's cheek!

But if I could only play one hole of golf one last time at the Patch, or heck maybe anywhere on the planet, it would be the old par 4 15th, which I would rank as the hardest hole in America. Sorry, number 12 at Augusta. You know I love you, and I have played you hundreds of times, but this is not in your category.

Short by any standard, yesterday's or today's, those 348 yards from tee to green at the Cabbage Patch's 15th are the longest I have ever known. Lined thick with oak trees and kudzu left and right, and a downward-sloping landing area the size of a dinner plate (and me without a knife and fork), the tee shot on 15 was without question the most challenging of the day. Frightening, might be the better word.

I'm a pretty good golfer and I sometimes get nervous, but I never get frightened, except on this hole.

The out of bounds access road at the Cabbage Patch taught me how to get back *in* bounds, and to always stay in bounds. And then, that road whispered in my ear and said—where is the fun in that? I'll see you out of bounds! That's where the fun is! (*Photo by Tripp Bowden*)

I've hit everything from driver to 9-iron off that tee. Yes, I've hit a 9-iron when I was guarding a really good round and didn't want to make a 10, or maybe even worse. Remember the kid from the beginning of this book that circled bogeys? Well, this was one of them.

Sadly, the 15th hole is long gone, lost in the wake of progress to make way for an Aquatic Center, of all things, although they did a mighty fine job with the facility. The once-feared landing area of the redesigned 15th is now wide enough to land a commercial jet, and the terraced green that wouldn't hold a lawn dart if you threw it down from the Moon, now sits benign and pancake-flat. Also gone is the old white cinder block clubhouse, with the old and young men drinking PBR and playing Gin Rummy in a beige-walled bathroom that doubled as a locker room. Gone, too, are Mr. Red and his lovely wife's chili dogs, and the Cokes with thin, crushed ice that you could chew and not worry about a trip to the dentist.

Gone too (though not far, to nearby UGA) is their youngest son, Jim, the first kid I ever saw break 80, with a set of Karsten 1s and ripping the balata (back when it was straight from the rubber tree) smack down the fairway time and time again, with a MacGregor Eye-O-Matic oil-hardened persimmon 2-wood, crafted in 1953.

A 2-wood, of all things!

Jim was a good dude. Still is, I reckon. I haven't talked to him in forever. He coaches the golf team at the University of Georgia, a Division I powerhouse. He's an assistant, has been from the get go, but embraces his role and plays it well. His kids love him and he can recruit like crazy.

It's funny the things you remember. And it's funny, the things you never forget. Sometimes, whenever I jingle whatever change I have in my pocket, Mr. Red and the memories of the Cabbage Patch come flooding back, and I hear them crashing not in the *back* of my mind but the *front*, wave on wave.

It is times like these when I think to myself: change is a good thing.

Acknowledgments

I'd like to thank the Academy.

I'm kidding. Even if I was ever up for an Oscar, I would *never* thank the Academy.

I would thank *you*, all of y'all who helped make this book happen, and to *you*, the folks who took time out of your busy lives to give it a gander. I hope you enjoyed these tales that run the gamut of the magical game of golf.

No offense to the Academy, but I'd much rather thank the folks who make the Academy happen. Because of all of y'all, this dream became a reality.

So here we go with my thank-yous, though they pale in comparison to your contributions.

To my wife, Fletch, I say thank you, thank you, for, well, there ain't no other way to say this but I gotta say it—for working your absolute ass off so I could take time from my daily duties (read: *steady income*) and try to make sense of what I believe is a really special story. The word "unique" comes to mind, which defines you, and this book, to a T. I love you, Fletch, more than you know and more than I show (it's time for me to fix that). I've never known a woman that comes close to comparing to you.

To my kiddos Holly Mac and Arrie B.—thank you for being so incredibly understanding when Daddy was under the gun, trying to make deadlines, and you wanted to kick around a soccer ball or dance together to Michael Jackson's "Smooth Criminal." I love y'all more than you will ever know, or maybe you do.

To good ol' Doctor Dave, who jump-started this collection of special golf tales on the beach at Fripp Island—was it the New Year's trip?—with the wind howling like Wolf Man Jack and me asking you to spill your guts about childhood, upbringing, and how the heck you knew the Hogan Way. Thank you, Doctor D., for your story from the heart. And thank you Kiki, dear wife of Doctor D., for holding down the fort. I love y'all.

Thank you, Cleopatrick, for your: *OK, Tripp, unconditional edits here they come.* Cleopatrick, you added so much life to these stories and, yes, you killed a darling or two, but in the end there was sunshine when your work was done.

To Jalik, for taking care of the kiddos and me when needed, while I put pen to paper. You've turned into a fine young man. Proud of you.

To my sister Jote, who long ago believed in my crazy ass no matter what, and was and still is the best dang sister a brother could ever dream of having. Thank you, Jote. And to my brother-in-law Toaster, all I can say is: party on, Wayne!

And I, Garth, shall party on, too.

And to my nephew Jarbs, well, thank you for being you, and for keeping my wheels on the road.

To my stepsister Nic: Thank you for reading the book when it was wearing just socks and undershorts (to paraphrase Stephen King), barely out the box, and for the magic you worked with the Cabbage Patch story. You told me I could do better, that I *must* do better, the first time you read the closing chapter then asked me for the beginning. I hope I have honored your 2016 summertime tutorial.

To my Mum—who read over this book when it was raw as a steak from the IGA, yet you praised me in spite of its weaknesses, thank you, Mum, from not just the bottom but the top of my heart. And to my Dad, Pop, a.k.a. Doc, who introduced me to the game and taught me the fundamentals, of golf and life. And to Mimi, who can play her arse off in spite of never, ever practicing. And also to my stepdad Peter, quite the writer in his own right, who encouraged me every step of the way.

To my editor, Julie Ganz, who worked absolute magic with my writing rabble-babble and was as patient as Job with all my back and forth. Her insight, kindness, and absoluteness are rare in life. Thank you, Julie, though the words "thank you" don't seem like quite enough.

God bless you, maybe?

And to Bill W., for giving me another shot at the bright lights and big city. And also to Johnny, Johnny, for first opening the Door, and Mark W., who long ago helped me walk through it. And to Bob Jones IV, my friend and fellow lover of the game, for penning the most beautiful foreword I have ever read.

Bub and Freddie are smiling down.

To everyone who told me their story of their most memorable round, I thank you for sharing your love of the game with me. For those whose story didn't make it into this book, I am feeling pretty good about a Volume II—fingers crossed. Hang tight, and we shall see.

There are *so* many wonderful golf stories out there, each as unique and different as snowflakes. Every golfer who loves the game like I do, like you do, has a special story to tell, and I can't wait to hear it.

Let's go catch those snowflakes on our tongue and be kids again! I'm at trippster@comcast.net. You can find me there.

Be safe, and love one another.

Tripp

PS Holly Mac and Arrie B? Daddy is ready to dance.